Contents

Introduction 10
unworthy and incompetent successors 10
Absence of any definite law of succession 10
Local and foreign Invasions on Delhi also made th 10
Rise of British 11
MINOR REASONS: 11
Expected Questions Topic1: 13
   Question No.1: 13
   Question No.2: 13
   Questions No.3: 13
   Questions No.4: 13
   Question No.5: 13
   Questions No.6: 13
   Question No.7: 13
   Question No.8: 13
   Question No.9: 14
   Question No.10: 14
   Question No.11: 14
   Question No.12: 14
   Question No.13: 14
MANSABDARI SYSTEM: 15
AURANGZEB'S DECCAN POLICY: 15
SUBSIDIARY ALLIANCE: 15
PARAMOUNTCY: 15
RELIGIOUS POLICY OF AURANGEB: 15
   Results of the religious policy of Aurangzeb: 17
   These conflicts were: 17
TOPIC 2 19
Introduction 19
BRITISH EXPANSION AND UNSUCCESSFUL INDIAN RESISENCE 1750-1850: 19
Battle of Buxar 20
Control South India 20
Afghanistan 20
Punjab 20
DOCTRINE OF LAPSE: 21
TIPU SULTAN: 21
RANJIT SINGH: 22
EXPECTED QUESTIONS : 22

Topic 3 25

SHAH WALLI ULLAH (1703-1762) 25

Early Biographical detail: 25

Beliefs: 25

Works: 26

    1.   Religious Services 26

    2.   Political Services : 26

    3.   Social Services : 27

    Third Battle of Panipat 1761: 27

EXPECTED QUESTIONS: 27

Topic 4 29

Early Biographical detail: 29

Beliefs: 29

Battles   Against Sikhs: 29

Expected Questions: 30

Biographical detail: 31

BELIEFS: 31

Services of Haji Shariat Ullah: 31

Death of Haji Shariat Ullah 31

Titu Mir: 32

EXPECTED QUESTIONS: 32

    The authority of the Mughal emperors was declining by the end of Aurangzeb's reign in 1707. The Hindus were unhappy with aspects of his reign and after his death, began to exercise greater control over parts of the sub-continent. As a result Muslim power and influence over India, which had been so strong, began to disintegrate. Many Muslims began to feel strongly about reviving Islam, including Haji Shariat Ullah. 32

COMPARISIONS OF RELIGIOUS THINKERS 33

    Analysis: 33

Topic 6 34

THE WAR OF INDEPENDENCE 1857: 34

    Economic cause: 34

    Social and religious cause 35

    POLITICAL CAUSES: 36

    MILITARY CAUSES : 36

Events of WOI: 36

    The war of Independence of 1857 achieved nothing 38

EXPECTED SHORT QUESTIONS:. 39

Expected Questions: 39

TOPIC 7: 41

    Early Biographical details: 41

Beliefs: 41

Educational Reforms/Aligarh College: 41

1859: Built Gulshan School in Muradabad. 42

Reconciliation Policy: 42

Political Reforms: 43

URDU HINDI CONTROVERSY 1867: 43

URDU 47

Key Points: 47

SINDHI 48

Key Points: 48

PASHTTO 49

Key points: 49

PUNJABI 50

Key points: 50

BALOCHI 51

PASTPAPERS QUESTIONS: 51

ANSWER TO QUESTION NO. 16: 53

Section 2 54

Introduction 54

Reasons for partition of Bengal 54

Muslims' Response 55

Hindus Response 56

Annulment of the Partition 56

Expected Question & Answers: 56

Answer to Question No. 2: 57

Answer to Question No. 6: 58

What   was the Simla Deputation? 60

Demands of Simla Deputation 60

Reasons for the formation of MUSLIM LEAGUE: 61

INDIAN NATIONAL CONGRESS: 61

Expected Questions & Answers: 62

Answer to Question No. 2 62

Introduction 63

main features of the Act of 1909 63

Expected Questions & Answers 64

Answer to question No 1: 64

ANSWER TO QUESTION NO. 2: 65

What was the Lucknow pact? 66

Why was the Lucknow pact made? 66

Muslims' New Strategy after reversal of partition of Bengal 66

Jinnah's Role and liberal leadership 66

Joint Demand 66

Main clauses of the Lucknow Pact 67

Importance of the Pact: 67

Expected Questions & answers: 68

The Montague Chelmsford Reforms (Indian Council Act 1919) 69

Introduction 69

Main features of the Act of 1919 69

INDIANS RESPONSE: 69

DIARCHY: 70

AMRITSAR MASSACRE 1919: 70

Introduction 71

Aims of Khilafat Movement 71

Khilafat conferences: 72

First Khilafat Conference: November 1919 in Delhi. 72

Second Khilafat Conference: 72

Mehmed VI : 72

MUSTAFA KAMAL ATATURK: 72

Expected Questions and Answers 74

Answer to question No. 9 76

TOPIC 15 77

JINNAH'S DEHLI PROPOSALS MARCH 1927: 77

THE SIMON COMMISSION 1927 77

NEHRU REPORT 1928 78

JINNAH'S 14 POINTS 1929: 79

KEY POINTS: 80

Expected Question & Answers: 80

Answer to Questions No 1 & 3: 82

Topic 16 83

Introduction 83

First Round Table Conference 83

Second Round Table Conference 85

Third Round Table Conference 86

SALT MARCH: 87

GANDHI-IRWIN PACT: 87

COMMUNAL AWARD: 87

Expected Questions & Answers 88

Answer to question No.4 & 10: 90

Answer to question No. 3 & 6: 92

Topic 17 93

Introduction 93

Key Points: 93

1937 ELECTIONS: 94

Expected Question & Answers: 95

Answer to Question no. 1: 96

Topic 18 96

Introduction 96

Congress Tyranny: 96

Expected Questions & Answer: 98

Answer to Question No. 2: 100

Introduction 102

Proceedings 102

The statement 102

Iqbal's Allahabad Address 1930: 104

Expected question & answer: 106

Answer to Question No.1: 107

Topic 20 109

Introduction 109

Contents of Cripps Mission: 109

Expected Questions & Answer 111

Answer to question no. 3: 111

QUIT INDIA MOVEMENT BY GANDHI 1942: 113

What in quit India campaign? 114

Expected question & answer: 115

Answer to Question No.1: 115

Topic 21 117

THE GANDHI – JINNAH TALKS 1944: 117

Expected Questions and Answer: 117

Answer to Question No.1: 117

CAUSES OF THE FAILURE OF SIMLA CONFERENCE: 120

Expected questions and answers: 121

Topic 23 124

CABINET MISSION PLAN 1946 124

Proposals of the cabinet mission plan: 125

DIRECT ACTION DAY 1946 126

THE 3RD JUNE PLAN 1947 126

Proposals of the 3rd June plan; 128

THE RADCLIFFE BOUNDARY AWARD 1947: 128

ACHIEVEMENT OFQUAID-E-AZAM 130

As a leader: 130

Building a Nation: 130

Building a government: 130

Building an economy: 131

Establishing national security: 132

Conclusion: 132

Expected questions: 132

TOPIC 24 134

Introduction: 134

Geographical problems: 134

Political problems: 134

Economic problems: 134

The percentage of economic assets in Pakistan after partition: 135

Electricity Problem 136

Social problems: 136

The accession of the princely states: 136

Hyderabad 136

Junagarh 137

The Kashmir Issue: 137

The division of financial and military assets: 138

The canal water dispute: 139

Refugees and the accommodation crises: 140

Drawbacks in Educational System: 140

Lack of proper planning: 140

Policies and their implementation: 140

Administrative set up: 141

Lack of funds: 141

Poor condition of Schools: 142

Teachers: 142

Examination System: 142

Expected questions: 142

ANSWER TO QUESTION NO. 4:- 145

Liaqat Ali khan 147

Objectives Resolution 147

Liaquat- Nehru Pact 147

Assassination 148

Khawaja Nazimuddin 148

Muhammad Ali Bogra, ... 148

Iskander Mirza 149

OBJECTIVE RESOLUTION 1949: 150

Public and Representative Officer's disqualification Act (PRODA): 151

One unit policy: 151

Expected Questions 152

Topic 26 153

POLITICAL AND CONSTITUTIONAL REFORMS: 153

    1959 Basic Democracies: 153

The 1962 Constitution: 153

    It stated that: 153

Election of 1965: 155

A New capital: 155

Agricultural reforms / the Green Revolution: 156

Industrial reforms: 156

Social and Educational reforms: 157

Political unrest and downfall of Ayub: 158

Expected Questions: 160

Introduction 162

KEY POINTS: 162

Results: 162

West Pakistan reacts: 163

The outbreak of Civil War: 164

War with India: 164

Reason for defeat: 165

Consequences of war: 165

Reasons for Separation of East Pakistan 1971: 165

SHEIKH MUJIB: 166

EXPECTED QUESTIONS: 166

Topic 28 166

Introduction 167

KEY POINTS: 167

    Political reforms: 167

    The Simla Agreement: 168

    Establishing a new constitution: 168

    Industrial Reforms: 168

    Problems for nationalization policy: 169

    Agricultural reforms: 169

    Education: 169

    Problems for new education policies: 170

    Health and Social Reforms: 170

Problems for health policies: 170

The 1977 elections: 170

Steps to downfall: 170

EXPECTED QUESTIONS: 171

Topic 29 172

Introduction 172

Islamisation under ZIA: 174

ECONOMIC REFORMS: 177

POLITICAL REFORMS: 178

Afghan War Settlement: 178

Mohammad Khan Junejo becomes PM 1985 to 1988: 178

EXPECTED QUESTIONS: 180

Topic 30: 182

Introduction 182

Nawaz sharif becomes PM 1990: 184

Reasons for Downfall: 185

Moin Qureshi as caretaker PM: 185

BB becomes PM1993: 185

Malik Meraj becomes caretaker PM 1996: 187

Nawaz Sharif as PM 1996: 188

Expected Questions: 189

Topic31 190

PAKISTAN'S FOREIGN RELATIONS: 190

UNITED NATIONS ORGANIATION: 190

General Assembly: 190

Security Council: 190

Economic and Social Council: 190

Trusteeship Council: 191

International Court of Justice: 191

ORGANIZTION OF ISLAMIC CONFERENCE (OIC): 191

INDIA PAKISTAN RELATIONS: 191

PAKISTAN AND MUSLIM COUNTRIES: 193

PAKISTAN AND BANGLADESH: 194

PAKISTAN AND IRAN: 195

PAKISTAN AND AFGHANISTAN: 196

PALESTINIAN ISSUE: 197

PAKISTAN AND EGYPT: 198

PAKISTAN AND USSR: 199

PAKISTAN, UNO AND UNITED STATES: 201

PAKISTAN AND BRITAIN: 202

REASONS FOR THE DECLINE OF THE MUGHAL EMPIRE 1707-1857:

Introduction

The Mughal Empire reached its greatest extent in the time of Aurangzeb Alamgir, but it collapsed with dramatic suddenness within a few decades after his death. The Mughal Empire owes its decline and ultimate downfall to a combination of factors; firstly Aurangzeb's religious policy is regarded as a cause for the decline of the Mughal Empire as it led to disunity among the INDIAN people.

unworthy and incompetent successors

Another reason was unworthy *and incompetent successors* of Aurangzeb. The character of Mughal kings had deteriorated over a period of time. The successive rulers after Aurangzeb were weak and lacked the character, motivation and commitment to rule the empire strongly. They had become ease loving and cowardly. They totally disregarded their state duties and were unable to detain the declining empire from its fall. These later Mughal rulers were absolutely incompetent and weak. They were proven neither *good generals nor good statesmen* who could control or administer the large empire which covered nearly the whole of the subcontinent during Aurangzeb's rule. The later rulers were also pleasure loving and were renowned for *living an extravagant lifestyle* with little thought to the effect it had on the economy of the empire. They also lacked courage, determination and training. Money was spent lavishly on fine buildings, jewellery, fine clothes and food. No infrastructure was created for the improvement of administration, industry or agriculture.

Absence of any definite law of succession

The *absence of any definite law of succession* was another important factor. The war of successions not only led to bitterness, bloodshed, and loss of money and prestige of the empire over a period of time, but to its eventual fall. Wars of succession were also an important reason. After the death of a ruler, the princess fought for the throne. This eroded the strength and led to the instability of the Mughal Empire. **Aurangzeb** fought against his brothers *Dara Shiko and Shuja*, and later got *Kamran* killed. Infighting continued even after Aurangzeb like *Moazzam* who succeeded the throne under the name of **Bahadur Shah** after Aurangzeb, defeated his brothers *Azam and Kam Baksh* and killed them. Bahadur Shah ruled for 5 years and died in 1712. His sons also fought for the throne. The infighting for the throne greatly weakened the Mughal Empire.

Local and foreign Invasions on Delhi also made the Mughals weak.

Marathas were the major opponents of Mughals. They were from central and south India. Aurangzeb fought with them but could not control them. Until 1750, they had become a major threat for the Mughals. However, Marathas were defeated in 1761 in the battle of Panipat and powerless Mughals got some more time to rule India. Besides Marathas, two more invasions took place from Afghanistan and Persia. In 1738, Persian General Nadir shah invaded Delhi and looted their wealth. Between 1747 and 1769, Afghan General Ahmed Shah invaded India ten times. Even in Punjab, Sikhs were also a major threat for the Mughals. All these invasions made the Mughals virtually bankrupt and they lost their power completely. Mughal Kingdom was reduced to an area 300 miles long and 100 miles wide near Delhi within 100 years after the death of Aurangzeb.

Rise of British

The **rise of British** power was the main reason of the decline of the Mughals. The British took full advantage of the weakness of the Mughals and gradually increased their power. The British expanded the territory under their control with the help of their superior administration and organization. A series of battles and annexations, through steps like '"**ubsidiary Alliance' and 'Doctrine of Lapse'** and effective administration the British gradually assumed control over a vast territory in the subcontinent. They also had clear military advantage because of **Industrial development** in England (1750-1850). The British had better weapons, superior war techniques and a well-trained and disciplined army. The British possessed a strong **naval** force .The result was that by 1803 the British took over Delhi and placed Shah Alam under British protection with a pension.

MINOR REASONS:

The degeneration of the rulers had also led to the **moral degeneration of the nobility**. Under the early Mughals, the nobles performed useful functions and distinguished themselves both in war and peace. But the elite under the later Mughals was more interested in worldly pursuit and self-enhancement. The nobles who had once been talented men with integrity, honesty, and loyalty, turned selfish and deceitful. Growth of hostile and rival clique in the court also undermined the strength of the government. Widespread **corruption** in the administration started and taking bribes became common.

One of the most potent causes of the fall of the Mughal Empire was the deterioration and _**demoralization of the army**_. The military had not only become inefficient but also lacked in training, discipline and cohesion. The army was out-dated in regard to equipment. It consisted of contingents maintained by various nobles, which was the main source of Army's weakness. As the weakening of the nobles occurred, so did the army. This was because of the soldiers, instead of identifying and uniting as Mughal Indians, identified themselves with different ethnic groups like Persian, Afghans and Central Asians. The Mughals had _**no navy**_ and only maintained small ships that were no match for the well- equipped ships of the foreign traders. It was this weakness that the French and the British used to their advantage, and were eventually able to establish their control over India

Another factor contributing to the decline was the _**financial position of the Mughals,**_ which had become deplorable. The war of successions, rebellions and luxurious style of living had depleted the once enormous treasury and had led to financial bankruptcy. During the time of Aurangzeb, the Mughal Empire had expanded to reach its maximum size. This **_vast area_** had become impossible for one ruler to control and govern from one centre. It was during the later Mughals that Deccan, Bengal, Bihar and Orissa declared their independence

Expected Questions Topic1:

Question No.1:
Was the infighting between Aurangzeb's successors the most important reason for the collapse of the Mughal Empire? Explain your answer.   (14) November 2001. (Q.1.c)

Question No.2:
Briefly explain three reasons for the decline of the Mughal Empire.   (7) June.2002.(Q.1.b)

Questions No.3:
"Aurangzeb's successors failed to live up to his courageous and determined personality". Was this the most important reasons for the decline of the Mughal Empire? Give reasons for your answer.

(14) November 2003 (Q.1.c)

Questions No.4:
Why were the British able to replace the Mughals as the dominant force in the Sub Continent by 1850?   (7) November 2004. (Q. 1.b)

Question No.5:
Were the weak and greedy characteristics of Aurangzeb's successors the most important reasons for the collapse of the Mughal Empire? Explain your answer.   (14)   November   2005. (Q.1.c)

Questions No.6:
Explain why the Mughal Empire declined following the reign of Aurangzeb.

(7) June 2006.(Q.1.b)

Question No.7:
"The coming of the British was the main reason for the decline of the Mughal Empire", do you agree or disagree? Give reasons for your answer.   (14)   June 2007(Q.1.c)

Question No.8:

Explain why the successors of Aurangzeb failed to prevent the decline of the Mughal Empire.

(7) November 2008 (Q.1.b)

Question No.9:
'The policies of Aurangzeb were the main reason for the decline of the Mughal Empire'. Do you agree or disagree? Give reasons for your answer.   (14)   November 2009(Q.1.c)

Question No.10:
The spread of Maratha power was the main reason for the decline of the Mughal Empire. Do you agree or disagree? Give reasons for your answer.   (14)   June   2011 (Q.1.c)

Question No.11:
Explain why the Mughal Empire declined following the reign of Aurangzeb.

(7) June 2012 (Q. 1.b)

Question No.12:
Read the source below carefully to answer question (a).
The Mughal Empire took 150 years from the death of Aurangzeb in 1707 to break up. His empire was facing difficulties at the time of his death and following this, the tensions and problems only became worse. The most serious challenge to Mughal authority came from the Marathas.
(a) Describe what the Marathas did. (4) June 2013 (Q.1.a)

Question No.13:
How did the successors of Aurangzeb contribute to the downfall of the Mughal Empire?

(7) November 2013 (Q.1.b)

MANSABDARI SYSTEM:

"Mansab" is an Arabic word which means a post, an officer a rank, or status. Therefore, Mansabdar means an officer or the holder of the rank, status, and post. Akbar introduced a new system for regulating imperial services which was called Mansabdari system. It was introduced in 1570 A. D. All the imperial officers of the state were styled as Mansabdars. They were classified into (66) grades, from the rank of (10) to ten thousands (10,000) constituted. The (10) was the lowest rank and the ten thousand (10,000) was the highest. The Mansabdars belonged to both Civil and Military department.

AURANGZEB'S DECCAN POLICY:

Aurangzeb spent the last 25 years of his life (1682-1707) in the Deccan. During all this long period, he had practically no rest. The object of his Deccan wars was to conquer the states of Bijapur & Golconda & crush the power of Marathas. But the Marathas did not submit themselves and continued their struggle till the end. Thus his 25 years of campaign in Deccan resulted in nothing. The wars in the Deccan drained his resources & loosened his grip in the north. This led to his tragic end in 1707 at Ahamadnagar and slowly led to downfall of Mughal Empire.

SUBSIDIARY ALLIANCE:

The doctrine of subsidiary alliance was introduced by Lord Wellesley, (1798-1805). According to this the Indian rulers were not allowed to have their own armed forces. They were protected by the company's forces but had to pay for them. If any ruler failed to make the payment, a part of his territory would be taken away.

PARAMOUNTCY:

Under Warren Hasting (1774-85), a new policy of paramount was initiated. The company claimed its authority was paramount or supreme as its power was greater than the Indian rulers. So they decided that they could annex or threaten to annex any state of India. It was applied by Lord Dalhousie in 1852. when a ruler didn't govern his state the British would annex his land. (Oudh, Nagpur)

RELIGIOUS POLICY OF AURANGEB:

1. **Demolishing temples and breaking idols :**Mosques were built at the sites of different temples

2. **Imposed Jaziya:** Akbar had abolished this tax on the Hindus but Aurangzeb again levied this tax. Aurangzeb issued very strict instructions to the officers regarding the collection of Jaziya.

3. Discriminatory toll fare: The Hindu traders were required to pay a toll tax of 5 per cent as against half of it paid by the Muslim traders. Later on Muslim traders were totally exempted from the payment of this tax.

4. Removal of the Hindus from Government jobs: Aurangzeb's predecessors, especially Akbar had appointed a large number of Hindus in the various departments, but Aurangzeb followed the policy of removal of the Hindus from these jobs. The Hindus were not allowed to occupy high administrative or executive posts. A general order prohibiting the employment of the Hindus in the revenue department was passed in 1670.

5. Restrictions on Hindu educational institutions: For destroying the culture of the Hindus, Aurangzeb destroyed their several educational institutions at Varanasi, Multan and Thatta. He placed restrictions on the starting of new pathshalas. The Hindu children were disallowed to study the fundamentals of their faith. They were not allowed to attend Muslim Madaras and Maqtabs.

6. Conversion through different means: For the Hindus the only way to escape from the payment of various taxes like pilgrim tax, trade tax, Jizya, etc. was conversion to Islam. Getting jobs after conversion also became easier. The Hindu prisoners were freed on their conversion to Islam. All sorts of promises were made to the converted.

7. Social restrictions: Aurangzeb issued order that except Rajputs, no Hindu could ride an elephant, a horse and a palanquin. Holi and Diwali festivals were allowed to be celebrated with certain restrictions. The Hindus could no longer put on fine clothes. The Hindus were not allowed to burn their dead on the banks of the river Sabarmati in Ahmedabad. Similar restrictions were placed at Delhi on the river Jamuna.

Results of the religious policy of Aurangzeb:

The religious fanaticism of Aurangzeb overshadowed his virtues. His reversal of Akbar's policy of religious toleration resulted in weakening the entire structure of the Mughal Empire. It led to several conflicts and wars in different parts of the country.

These conflicts were:

(i)   Conflict with the Jats
(ii)   Conflict with the Satnamis
(iii)   Conflict with the Sikhs
(iv)   Conflicts with the 'ajput's
(v)   Conflict with the Marathas.

All these rebellions destroyed the peace of the empire, disrupted its economy, weakened the administrative structure, and diminished its military strength, led to the failure of Aurangzeb to make any impact. Ultimately all these contributed to the downfall of the Mughal enterprise.

The Mughal Family Line

Babur
- **Humayun** | Askari Mirza | Hindal Mirza | Gulrukh Begum | Kamran Mirza
- **Akbar** | Muhammad Hakim
- **Jahangir** | Khanzada Khanim | Shah Murad | Danyal | Shakarunnisa Begum | Aram Banu Begum
- Sultan Nisar Begum | Khurasw | Parvez | Bahar Banu Begum | **Shahjahan** | Shahrayar | Jahandar
- Dara Shikoh | Shah Shuja | Jahanara Begum | Rawsha-nara Begum | **Aurangzib** | Murad Bakhsh

Reasons for the arrival of the EIC in the Sub Continent:

Introduction

The main prospects which attracted Britain was certainly trade and for that the British East India Company was founded in 1600 with the permission to **trade** with India. The first British ship anchored near Surat in 1608. They were also granted permission by the Mughals to trade in 1612. The British established their headquarters in Bombay in 1674 and at Calcutta in 1690. Main trading items were cotton and silk textiles, spices, tea, indigo, precious stones and salt peter.

S.M Burk (famous historian) believed that one of the most important reasons for British arrival was the spreading of **Christianity** .Churches and Chapels were established all over India and Christian missionaries also began with their arrival.

The **Portuguese** and the **Dutch** were already in the field. But they turned their attention to East **Indies** and didn't allow EIC to come over there. That also provoked company to come here in India. The French also came but they were eliminated after their defeat by the British in 3 battles.

Therefore it was trade and **high profit** that allowed the EIC to keep on coming India which was later also known as the Golden Sparrow on account of its natural resources and wealth. It was found that 10% of the income of British government was obtained from taxes on trade with India.

Another reason which provoked Britain to come towards India was the **Russian expansion** in Central Asia. It worried the British so much that they also had to make moves to secure Afghanistan. Although the British first major adventure in Afghanistan in 1839 failed miserably, but in 1858, after the failure of the war of Independence 1857, the British assumed full and proper control of whole of India.

BRITISH EXPANSION AND UNSUCCESSFUL INDIAN RESISENCE 1750-1850:

The British were almost completely successful in taking control of lands in the S.C between 1750 and 1856. The British had come to India for trade and to increase and ensure their trade they found it necessary to have political control of lands in the sub-continent. The first opportunity came in 1757 when battle of Plassey took place. In this battle the forces of the East India Company under **Robert Clive** met the army of **Siraj-ud-Doula**, the Nawabs of Bengal. Clive had 800 Europeans and 2200 Indians whereas Siraj-ud-doula in his entrenched camp at Plassey was said to have about 50,000 men with a train of heavy artillery. Unfortunately **Mir Jafar,** met with Clive, and the greater number of the Nawabs soldiers were bribed to throw away their weapons, surrender prematurely, and even turn their arms against their own army. Siraj-ud-Doula was defeated. Battle of Plassey marked the first major military success for British East India Company.

Battle of Buxar

It was followed by battle of **Buxar. Mir Kasim** the Nawab of Bengal took help from **Nawab Shuja-ud-daulah** and the Emperor **Shah Alam II**. But the English under the **General Major Hector Munro** at Buxar defeated the combined army on 22 October, 1764. Mir Kasim fled and died in 1777. After winning the Battle of Buxar, the British had earned the right to collect land revenue in Bengal, Bihar and Orissa. This development set the foundations of British political rule in India. After the victory of

the English in Buxar, **Robert Clive** was appointed the governor and commander in chief of the English army in Bengal in 1765. He is claimed as the founder of the British political dominion in India. Robert Clive also brought reforms in the administration of the company and the organization of the army.

Control South India

The British wanted full control of south India to ensure their spice trade. **Lord Wellesley** became the Governor General of India in 1798. **Tipu Sultan** tried to secure an alliance with the French against the English in India. Wellesley questioned Tipu's relationship with the French and attacked Mysore in 1799. The fourth Anglo-Mysore War was of short duration and decisive and ended with Tipu's death on May 4, 1799 who was killed fighting to save his capital.

Besides that Marathas were also defeated and Maratha power destroyed by British in several wars during 1817- 1818. **Holkar's** forces were routed at Mahidpur December 21, 1817 and **Baji Rao II**, who was trying to consolidate Marathas, finally surrendered in June 1818. British abolished the position of Peshwa and Marathas were limited to the small kingdom of Satara. This ended the mighty Maratha power.

Afghanistan

British wanted to make sure that Afghanistan didn't fall into Russian hands. British agreed with Ranjit Singh (ruler of Punjab) that Afghanistan should remain independent. A rebellion broke out in Afghanistan in 1841 in which British troops were killed. British felt that their pride had been hurt in Afghanistan and decided to turn in Sindh. Sindh was ruled by collection of **Amirs** who had signed a treaty with British in 1809. British General **Sir Charles Napier** provoked the Amirs of Sindh so much that they attacked British residency in 1843. Amirs were defeated and Sindh was annexed by British.

Punjab

Punjab was the next target. Ranjit Singh had signed a perpetual friendship in 1809 but after his death in 1839, the rival chiefs argued themselves over who should be a king. Army attacked British possessions south of River Sutlej and provoked the British to invade Punjab .War began but British remained victorious. Gulab Singh Dogra, a chief who helped the British and was given Kashmir as a reward. In 1849, after a revolt against British, Punjab, NWFP were annexed and became part of British Empire on 30 March 1849. Hyderabad, Deccan, Oudh and the local Nawabs had been forced to sign treaties with EIC; this gave their external affairs to Britain.

DOCTRINE OF LAPSE:

In 1852, the British annexed several Indian states under doctrine of lapse. In 1852 Governor **General Dalhousie** extended British control by applying Doctrine of Lapse which was that when a ruler died without a natural heir, the British would annex his lands. Due to this Satare, Nagpur and Jhansi came to British hands. Nawab of Oudh died in 1856 and he had the natural heir but instead of that his land was grabbed by the British.

TIPU SULTAN:

Tipu Sultan (20 November 1750 – 4 May 1799), also known as the **Tiger of Mysore** and **Tipu Sahib** ,was a ruler of the Kingdom of Mysore and a scholar, soldier, and poet. He was the eldest son of Sultan Hyder Ali of Mysore. Tipu introduced a number of administrative innovations during his rule, including his coinage, and a new land revenue system which initiated the growth of Mysore silk industry. Tipu expanded the iron-cased Mysorean rockets and wrote the military manual Fathul Mujahidin, considered a pioneer in the use of rocket artillery. He deployed the rockets against advances of British forces and their allies in their 1792 and 1799. In the Fourth Anglo-Mysore War, the combined forces of the British East India Company and the Nizam of Hyderabad defeated Tipu, and he was killed on 4 May 1799 while defending his fort of Srirangapatna.

RANJIT SINGH:

Maharaja Ranjit Singh (13 November 1780 – 27 June 1839) was the founder of the Sikh Empire, which came to power in the Indian subcontinent in the early half of the 19th century. The empire, based in the Punjab region, existed from 1799 to 1849. Ranjit Singh was succeeded by his son, Kharak Singh.

EXPECTED QUESTIONS :

Question No.1: Why did the East India Company become involved in the India Sub continent?

(7) June 2001 Q.1 b

Question No.2: How successful was Indian resistance to British attempts to take control of Lands in the Sub Continent? Explain your answer.   (14) June 2002 Q.1c

Question No.3: Why did the British government take control of the affairs of the East India Company in the early 19th century?   (7) June 2004 Q.1b

Question No. 4: Why were the British able to replace the Mughals as the dominant force in the sub- continent by 1850?   (7) November 2004 Q.1b

Question No.5: Explain why the East India Company became involved in the Indian sub-continent during the 17th century.   (7) June 2005 Q.1 b

Question No. 6: Why was Britain so successful in expanding its control of the sub-continent between 1750 and 1850?   (7) November 2006 Q.1 b

Question No. 7: Why did the Indian Sub-Continent attract European traders in the late 16th and early 17th centuries?   (7) June 2007, Q.1 b

Question No.8: Indian resistance to British attempts to take control of lands in the S.C was totally unsuccessful. Do you agree? Give reasons for your answer.   (14) June 2008, Q.2 c

Question No.9: why was Britain successful in increasing its control of some parts of the S.C in the years 1750 to 1850?   (7) June 2009, Q.2 b

Question No.10: Explain why the East India Company got involved in the S.C during the

17th Century? (7) June 2009, Q.1
b

Question No.11: with the slow crumbling of the Mughal Empire, the only question left in

the early 18th century was who would pick up the pieces. Few observers could have guessed

that the EIC would have played such a major role.

What was the East India Company? (4) June 2010, Q.1.a

Question No.12: Why did EIC become involved in the Indian S.C during the 17th Century?
(7)
November 2010 Q.1 b

Question No.13: how successful were the British attempts to take control of lands in the S.C
between 1750 and 1856? (14) November 2010 Q.1 c **Question No.14:** Explain why Britain was
so successful in extending its control of the S.C between 1750

and   1850. (7) June 2011, Q.1 b
Question No.15: In 1756 the French encouraged the nawab of Bengal, siraj ud daula to attack east

India Company's base at Calcutta. He captured the city but was unable to keep control of it.

Robert Clive decided to go to the city with a force of soldiers to retake it. This led to the battle

of plassey.

Describe the battle of plassey. (4) June 2012, Q.1 a

Question No.16: How successful was Indian resistance to British attempts to take control of
Lands in the Sub-Continent between 1750 and 1850? Explain your answer. (14) November
2012 Q.1c

Question No.17: Why was Britain successful in maintaining its control of the sub-continent in
the years 1750 to 1850?
[7] June 2013 Q.2 b

Question No.18: Was the Industrial Revolution in Britain the most important reason why the
British were able to take control of India between 1750 and 1850? Explain your answer.
[14] November 2013 Q.1 c

Question No. 19: Explain why the East India Company became involved in the sub-continent
during the seventeenth century. [7] May/June 2014

Q.1 b

Question No.20: At first the East India Company had a neutral point of view towards religion in India. However, with the work of missionaries in the sub-continent, the Christian faith of British people living in India was strengthened. As a result people became more intolerant of Indian traditions and behaviour and the British began to impose changes on the way Indians lived, which caused resentment and anxiety.

What was suttee?   [4] Oct Nov 2014 Q.1

SHAH WALLI ULLAH (1703-1762)

Early Biographical detail:

Shah Wali Ullah Muhaddis Dehlvi was born on **February 21, 1703 at Delhi**, just when the reign of Aurangzeb was nearing its end. He was named **Qutb-ud-Din**, but is better known by his title of Wali Ullah, given to him by virtue of his goodness and piety. His **father, Shah Abdul Rahim**, was a sufi and theologian of great repute. He was the founding member and teacher of the **Madrasa-i-Rahimiyah** in Delhi and also taught there for 12 years. He was influenced by **Sheikh Abu Tahir bin Ibrahim**, a renowned scholar of the time.

Beliefs:

Shah Wali Ullah believed that Islam has lost its purity in the subcontinent. Hindu customs, practices and beliefs had crept into the worships and lives of the Muslims. It had become very important to tell the Muslims what was Islamic and what were simply myths and traditions.

During the reign of SWU, Mughal/Muslim rule declined sharply. He believed that the real cause of Muslims' decline was their ignorance from the teachings of Quran and Sunnah. He wanted the Muslims to implement Islamic teachings in all spheres of their lives – social, political, economic and religious. This would enable them to restore their pride and improve their living conditions.

He also believed that a number of social evils had corrupted the Islamic society. He wanted to transform the society in the light of Islamic teachings. He wanted the rulers to enforce Islamic laws e.g. Islam condemns social injustice and protects the rights of peasants and workers. He urged the rich Muslims to lead pure life and stay away from luxury and extravagance. He also urged the traders to follow Islamic laws in their dealings. He wanted to eradicate the sectarian differences that were undermining the foundations of Muslim unity.

Shah Wali Ullah wanted to protect Muslim religion, identity, values and interests. He believed that under the influence of infidels, Muslims will forget Islam and with the passage of time it would become difficult to distinguish them from non-Muslims. He therefore wished to revive the teachings of Quran and Sunnah in the subcontinent.

Works:

1. Religious Services

Shah Wali-Ullah rendered many religious services. He completed **the translation of Holy Quran** in **Persian** in 1738. Later on his sons Shah Rafi-ud-Din and Shah Abdul Qadir translated the Holy Quran in Urdu. Moreover Shah Wali-Ullah wrote **commentary on Ahadiths** in Arabic and Persian. Shah Wali-Ullah also arranged the Hadith in respect of their topics. In addition he worked for the renaissance of Islam and wrote **51 books**. He propagated that Islam was a universal power and thus the Muslims should be the dominant force in the Sub-Continent and elsewhere.

Shah Wali-Ullah also trained students in different branches of Islamic knowledge. He recommended the application **of Ijtihad** against blind Taqlid in his famous work **-al-Ijtihad wa-al-Taqlid.**

He studied the writings of each school-of-thought to understand their point of view, and then wrote comprehensive volumes about what is fair and just in light of the teachings of Islam. He adopted an analytical and balanced approach towards four major school-of-thought of mysticism. In order to create a balance between the four schools i.e. **Hanafi, Malaki, Shafii, Hambali** he wrote **Al-Insaf**.

2. Political Services :

Shah Wali-Ullah possessed a deep political insight. He tried to trace the causes of the decline of Mughal Empire. In the middle of the 18th century **Marathas** had become a great political power. They were threatening to occupy the crown of Delhi. At this critical juncture Shah Wali-Ullah in order to check their advance prepared **Najid-ullah** (Rohilla Chief) and **Shuja-ud-Daulah** (Nawab of Oudh) for **Jihad**. Moreover he wrote a letter to **Ahmed Shah Abdali**, King of Afghanistan requesting him to save the Muslims from the aggression of Marathas. Consequently in the **Third Battle of Panipat**, Ahmed Shah Abdali inflicted a crushing defeat on the Marathas. Marhattas were a constant threat to the crumbling Mughal Empire. Shah Wali Ullah tried to reconcile the basic differences amongst the different sections of the Muslims and considered the government as an essential means and agency for regeneration of the community. He wrote to Ahmad Shah Abdali; "*...give up the life of ease. Draw the sword and do not to sheath it till the distinction is established between true faith and infidelity...*"

In his time **Shias and Sunnis** were aggressively hostile to each other and their rivalry was damaging the Muslim unity. Shah wali ullah wrote **Izalat-al-Akhifa and Khilafat-al-Khulafa** in order to remove misunderstanding between Shias and Sunnis. He refused to denounce Shias as heretics.

In short, the Muslim Renaissance Movement launched by Shah Wali-Ullah was the forerunner of all the future freedom movements of Indo-Pakistan. Maulana Mohammad Qasim founder of Madressah Deoband and Sir Syed Ahmed Khan were among his followers. Later on his son Shah Abdul Aziz founded the Jihad Movement which was carried forward by Syed Ahmed Shaheed.

3. Social Services:

Shah Wali-Ullah directed his teachings towards reorienting the Muslim society with the concepts of basic **social justice**, removing social inequalities, and balancing the distribution of wealth. He established several branches of his school at Delhi for effective application of his ideas. In his book **"Hujjat-ullah-il- Balighah",** he pinpointed the causes of chaos and disintegration of Muslim society. He advised the Muslims to give up extravagance and wasteful expenditure on marriages, deaths, births and other occasions. Wealthy Muslims were asked to look after the poor and the needy.

Briefly speaking, Shah Wali-Ullah was responsible for awakening in the community the desire to win back its moral fervor and maintain its purity. To rescue a community's conscience, belief and faith from destruction was no small achievement. Even after his death in 1762, his sons and followers carried on his work and noble mission. Many future Islamic leaders and thinkers were inspired by his example.

Third Battle of Panipat 1761:

Mughal emperor Aurangzeb (1658–1707) was a devout Muslim and persecutor of Hindus. Hindus of the Deccan rallied around a charismatic leader named Shivaji who was proclaimed king of the Marathas in 1674. His movement continued to gain momentum after his death in 1680, reaching its zenith in the mid- 18th century when the Marathas Confederacy controlled lands extending from Hyderabad in the south to Punjab in the north. But the quest for a restored Hindu empire in India came to an end in 1761 when the Marathas were badly defeated by Afghan forces under Ahmed Shah Durani at the Third Battle of Panipat. Although the Afghans retreated from India, the Maratha Confederacy never recovered. The British East India Company was the beneficiary and got strength.

EXPECTED QUESTIONS:

Question No. 1: How important was the work of Shah Wali Ullah to the revival of Islam in the Sub- Continent? Explain your answer.   (14) Nov. 2000. Q. 1c

Question No. 2: Which of the following was the most important in the spread of Islam during 17th and 18th centuries.

   a) Shah wali Ullah
   b) Syed Ahemd Shaheed Barailvi
   c) Hai Shariat Ullah?

Explain your answer with reference to all three of the above.   (14) June 2001 Q.2c

Question No. 3: Why did Shah Wali Ullah wish to revive Islam in the Sub-Continent?

(7)June2003,Q.1b

Question No. 4: How important was S.W.U in the spread of Islam in the Sub-Continent before 1850? Explain your answer.   (14)Nov.2004,Q.1c

Question No. 5: Why did S.W.U have such an important influence on the revival of Islam in the Sub- Continent?
(7) Nov. 2005 Q. Ic

Question No. 6: Was the work of S.W.U the most important factor in the revival of Islam in the Sub- Continent during the 17th and 18th centuries? Give reason for your answer.

(14) Nov. 2006 Q.1 c

Question No. 7: Why were there attempts to revive Islam in the Sub-Continent during the 18th and early 19thcenturies?
(7)Nov.2007Q.1b

Question No.8: did SWU contribute more to the spread of Islam than anyone else in the sub-continent before 1850? Explain your answer.   (14)Nov.2009Q.2c

Question No.9: why did Shah Wali Ullah have such a major influence on the revival of Islam in the sub continent? (7) June2010Q.1b

Question No.10: By the end of Aurangzeb's reign the authority of the Mughal emperors was declining. Hindus were not happy with his reign and after his death, Muslim power and influence over India, which had been so strong, began to disintegrate. At this time SWU was growing up.

Describe the achievements of SWU in reviving Islam.   (4)June2011Q.1a

Question No.11: In 1756, the French encouraged the Nawab of Bengal, Siraj-ud-Daulah, to attack the East India Company's base at Calcutta. He captured the city but was unable to keep control of it. Robert Clive decided to go to the city with a force of soldiers to retake it. This led to the battle of Plassey.

Describe the battle of Plassey.   (4)June2012Q.1a

Question No.12: Who of the following was the most important in the spread of Islam during the seventeenth and eighteenth centuries:
(i) Shah Wali Ullah;
(ii) Syed Ahmad Shaheed Barailvi;
(iii) Hajji Shariat Ullah?
Explain your answer with reference to all three of the above.
(14) June 2013 Q.1 c

Topic 4

SyedAhmedShaheedBarelvy(1786-1831)

Early Biographical detail:

Syed Ahmed Shaheed was born **at Rai Bareilly** in November **1786.** His father **Shah Ilm-Ullah** was pious religious scholar. He was a well-built young man and took interest in manly sports. He was inspired spiritually by **Shah Abdul Aziz**. In 1810 he joined the army **of Nawab Ameer Khan of Tonak** in order to take part in **Jihad** against the British. He fought against the English and Sikh forces and displayed his skill in the art of fighting. Syed Ahmed Shaheed was an outstanding orator. His religious and political sermons won him many companions which included Shah Ismail and Shah Abdul Haye.

Beliefs:

In the first half of the nineteenth century Punjab was under the rule of Sikhs who were very cruel to the Muslims. They were showing disregard to the Muslim culture, customs and religious places The Sikh rule which extended from Punjab up to Kabul was harsh on Muslims. Mosques were dishonored & Muslims could not follow their religion freely.

On hearing about these brutalities Syed Ahmed Shaheed decided to launch Jihad against the Sikhs. For this purpose he founded Jihad Movement. The Muslims of India responded to his call and thousands of Muslims got themselves enrolled in the Jihad Movement. Syed Ahmed Shaheed decided to launch Jihad from North West Frontier region of the country. Thus on 17th January 1826 he started his journey along with thousands of Mujahideens. He reached Sindh via Gwalior, Tonak, Ajmer and Marwar. Then he went to Afghanistan through Balochistan. From Afghanistan he arrived at Nowshera after nine months journey.

Battles   Against   Sikhs:

On his arrival in the Frontier province the warriors of **Yousaf Zai** tribe, followers of Pir Syed Akbar Shah and the local Muslims joined **the Jihad Movement**. Syed Ahmed Shaheed declared war against Sikhs. Ranjit Singh the Sikh ruler of Punjab sent **Budh Singh** at the head of ten thousand soldiers to meet the challenge of the Mujahideens. **On 21st December 1826** a strong group of Mujahideens attacked the Sikh army at night. As a result thousands of Sikh soldiers were killed and Budh Singh had to retreat with heavy losses. Later on after several skirmishes the Sikh army was defeated in the battle of **Hazru**. After these successes Syed Ahmed Shaheed decided to organize the local administration. He established an Islamic state in the area and announced his caliphate on January 11, 1827. These victories and successes of Mujahideens disturbed Ranjit Sikh very much. He decided to weaken the Mujahideens through diplomacy. He reached Peshawar and won the sympathies of two local chiefs **Yar Mohammad Khan and Sultan Mohammad Khan** by appointing them the ruler of Peshawar. Thus the Muslims were divided into two camps. However Syed Ahmed Shaheed succeeded in conquering **Peshawar in November 1830**. Through mistake Syed Ahmed Khan re appointed Sultan Mohammad Khan the ruler of Peshawar. Unfortunately Sultan Mohammad turned a traitor and hatched a conspiracy against Syed Ahmed Shaheed. Thousands of Mujahideens were murdered treacherously at Peshawar (after the withdrawal of SASB to Balakot to liberate Kashmir). In the meantime Sikh army under **Sher Singh** advanced against the Mujahedeen. Syed Ahmed Shaheed gathered all of his forces and encamped at Balakot which was a very secure place. Sardar Sher Singh too arrived at **Balakot at** the head of 20 thousands soldiers. The Sikh army besieged the area. The famous *battle of Balakot* was fought on **6th May 1831.** The Sikhs emerged victorious. Almost all the Mujahideens including Syed Ahmed Shaheed were martyred.

Expected Questions:

Question No. 1: why did Syed Ahmed Shaheed Barelvi conduct a Jihad against the Sikhs in the early 19th century? (7)

November 2000, Q.1 b

Questions No. 2: why did Syed Ahmed Shaheed wish to revive Islam in the Sub-Continent? (7)
November 2002, Q.1b

Question No.3: Why did Syed Ahmed Shaheed have such a major influence on the revival of Islam in the Sub-Continent? (7)
November 2003, Q.1 b

Question No.4: Was the work of Syed Ahmed Shaheed the most important factor in the revival of Islam in the sub-continent during the 17th & 18th centuries? Give reasons for your answer. (14)
June 2008, Q.1

TOPIC: 5
Haji Shariat Ullah (1781-1840)

Biographical detail:

Haji Shariatullah was born in Faridpur **district of Bengal, in 1781**. He was the son of an ordinary farmer. After getting his early education from his village, he went to Arabia to perform Hajj at an early age of 18 years. He stayed there from 1799 to 1818 and got his religious education. He learnt Arabic and Persian from his teacher, **Maulana Basharat**. During his stay in Arabia he came into close contact with **Wahabism** started by **Muhammad bin Abdul Wahab**. On his return to Bengal he sought to purify Islam that was impaired by the Hindu influence.

BELIEFS:

He believed that the miserable condition of the Muslims in India led to the country being Dar-Ul-Harb (Country under Foreign Rule). He told that Friday prayer and Eid prayer cannot be offered here. He also believed that Muslim community had moved away from Islamic practice. He wanted them to return to what he thought was the proper observation of Islamic duties called Faraizi. This was why he started his movement was called Faraizi Movement. The Faraizi Movement supported the idea of Jihad against the non-Muslims who were undermining the true principles of Islam.

Services of Haji Shariat Ullah:

Haji Shariatullah awakened the Muslims of Bengal by initiating **the Faraizi Movement**. He started his movement among the most depressed section of the Muslim society; the farmers and the artisans. He called upon the people **to discard un-Islamic practices and customs, and to act upon the commandments of faith, the "Faraiz", or duties**. He requested them to **observe strictly the principles of faith and rules of Shariah, and to refrain from Hindu practices.** This movement was mainly religious and social in character. The growing popularity of the movement amongst the people of Bengal alarmed the Hindu landlords who stressed Haji Shariatullah. British and Hindu Landlords did not want Haji Shariat Ullah to create difficulty for them by uniting a desire to improve their lives and purify their religion so they drove Haji out of the reign to Nawabganj in Dhaka where he died in 1840

Death of Haji Shariat Ullah

After the **death of Haji Shariatullah in 1840**, his son, **Muhammad Mohsin**, popularly known as **Dadhu Mian,** organized the movement and carried on the work of his father. He also visited Arabia at an early age but was more politically active than his father. **Dadhu Mian** popularized and strengthened the movement by organizing it in a systematic way. He acquired great influence amongst the Muslim peasants and craftsmen of Dhaka, Faridpur and Pabna districts. He **appointed Khalifahs** who kept him informed about everything in their jurisdiction. Dadhu Mian vehemently **opposed the taxes** imposed by the landlords on Muslim peasants for the decoration of the image of *Durgah*. He asked his followers to settle in lands managed by the government. During the revolt of 1857, he was put under arrest for organizing the peasants of Faridpur districts against the British government. He went further to declare a Jihad against British government. The British arrested him & put him in prison. After his death in 1860, the *Fraizi* movement was declined.

Titu Mir:

Mir Nasir Ali, known as Titu Mir is another important figure who was moved by the sufferings of the Muslim of Bengal. After returning from Pilgrimage, Titu Mir devoted himself to the cause of his country. He made Narkelbaria, a village near Calcutta, the center of his activities. Many oppressed Muslim peasants gathered round Titu Mir in their resistance against the Hindu landlord, Krishna Deva Raj. Titu Mir was able to defeat Krishna Deva and set up government. The British aiding the Hindu landlords sent an army of 100 English Soldiers and 300 sepoys to Narkelbaria. In 1831, Titu Mir died fighting the British forces.

The death of Titu Mir did not dishearten his followers. His example rather served as a source of inspiration for them in the years to come.

EXPECTED QUESTIONS:

QUESTION NO. 1:- Who was TiTu Mir?   (4) Nov. 2011 Q.1 a

QUESTION NO. 2:- Did Haji Shariat Ullah contribute more to the spread of Islam than anyone else in the sub-continent before 1850? Explain your answer.

(14) Nov. 2011 Q.2 c

QUESTION NO. 3:- Who of the following was the most important in the spread of Islam during the seventeenth and eighteenth centuries:
i.   Shah Wali Ullah;
ii.   Syed Ahmad Shaheed Barailvi;
iii. Hajji Shariat Ullah?
      Explain your answer with reference to all three of the above.   **(14) June 2013 Q.1 c**

QUESTION NO.4:
   1 Read the source below carefully to answer question (a)
The authority of the Mughal emperors was declining by the end of Aurangzeb's reign in 1707. The Hindus were unhappy with aspects of his reign and after his death, began to exercise greater control over parts of the sub-continent. As a result Muslim power and influence over India, which had been so strong, began to disintegrate. Many Muslims began to feel strongly about reviving Islam, including Haji Shariat Ullah.
   (a) Describe the achievements of Haji Shariat Ullah in reviving Islam   **(4) Oct/Nov 2013 Q. 1 a**

COMPARISIONS OF RELIGIOUS THINKERS

Islam was widely spread in subcontinent by Shah Wali Ullah Syed Ahmed Shaheed Barelvi and Haji Shariat Ullah.

Shah Wali Ullah was a religious scholar. He taught Islamic teachings in the Madrassa Rahimya. This produced a number of scholars in the sub-continent and therefore increased spread of Islam. Shah Wali Ullah also translated the Quran in Persian. Arabic was not very much understood in the sub-continent so translating Quran revived Quranic teachings in the subcontinent because Muslims and also other people could understand Quranic teachings. Shah Wali Ullah also wrote to all Muslim leaders in the subcontinent to unite and defeat the Marathas it was partly due to his persuade that Ahmed Durrani came to subcontinent and defeated the Marathas. Thus by writing letters he decreased the non-Muslim influence of Marathas and united Muslim leaders which revived Islam in subcontinent. Shah Wali Ullah wrote several books about 51. These books were extremely popular. These not only converted many people to Islam and increase understanding of religion for Muslims of Islam but also united the different Muslim sectarian such as the Shias and Sunnis. Although SWU was the great scholar and revivalist but he was not completely successful in bringing Muslim power back to subcontinent and Muslims were still being oppressed by Marathas who prevented them from obeying there religions law.

Besides SWU, Syed Ahmed Shaheed Barelvi also played an important part in reviving Islam. He started the Jihad Movement. The Jihad Movement was a Movement started by Muslims to defeat the non- Muslim oppressors. The Movement united all the different Muslim against one common enemy (Sikhs). This showed the power of the Muslims and united the Muslim community which spread Islam. He was the man of action rather than scholar. He defeated Sikhs in many battles but in his last battle because of the treachery of local tribal lords he met with death in his last battle of balakot in 1831.

Haji Shariat Ullah was another great scholar and decided to start the Faraizi Movement. It indicated that Muslims should return to their religious teaching and perform their religious obligations. This particularly became popular in Bengal and Muslims were revived back to their religious teachings. His movement also united the Muslims of Bengal. However Faraizi movement also failed.

Haji Shariat Ullah could only bring rejuvenation in Bengal and so could not reach the entire subcontinent.

Analysis:

Although every religious thinker was quite successful in spreading the message amongst the people, Shah Wali Ullah through writings, Syed Ahmed Shaheed Barelvi through his Jihad Movement and Haji Shariat Ullah through his Faraizi movement, yet in my opinion Shah Wali Ullah was most successful as his work was ever lasting and sowed a seed for the later "Pakistan Movement".

Topic 6

THE WAR OF INDEPENDENCE 1857:

The revolt of 1857 was the most severe outburst of anger and discontent accumulated in the hearts of various sections of the Indian society ever since the inception of British rule in Bengal, following the Battle of Plassey in 1757 and the Battle of Buxar 1764. British historians called it a "**Sepoy Mutiny**" and the Indian historians termed it as the "*First War of Independence*". Jawaharlal Nehru in his book "Discovery of India" described it as the Feudal Revolt of 1857 and added that "it was much more than a military mutiny and it rapidly spread and assumed the character of a popular rebellion and a war of Indian Independence".

Though the revolt was started by the Indian soldiers in the service of the East India Company, it soon proliferated all over the country. Millions of peasants, artisans and soldiers fought heroically for over a year and sacrificed their life so that others might live. Hindus and Muslims kept their religious differences aside and fought together in order to free themselves from foreign subjugation.

The British tried to dismiss this Revolt by merely calling it a "Sepoy Mutiny", but this Revolt clearly shows the hatred that the Indians had for the foreigners. The Revolt did not take place overnight. There were many causes that added fuel to the fire. The British were exploiting the Indians and the following reasons led to revolt.

Economic cause:

a) The first two hundred years (sixteenth and seventeenth centuries) the East India Company confined its activities to trade and commerce and had no political intention. The production of the Indian goods became so popular that the **British government had to pass a law in 1720 forbidding the use of Indian textiles.**

During the 18th century, the pattern of trade went through a drastic change. *With the advent of the Industrial Revolution, England developed its own textile industry and with that the dependence on Indian textiles came to an end. Demand for Indian textiles having reduced, the local handloom industry faced heavy losses and suffered badly.*

Gradually, the Indian handicraft and Cottage industries died out. There was major *unemployment* problem and that resulted in resentment among workers against the British rule. *The little patronage that they received from the native princes also was gone because of the annexations of those dominions.* The miserable condition of the working class led to this rebellion against the British Rule. The *trade and commerce of the country was monopolized by the by the East Indian Company*. No efforts were made to improvise on the living conditions of the people. Cruel exploitation of the economic resources made people miserable leading to periodic famines.

b) The **British confiscated the lands and properties of many landlords.** These landlords became leaders of the Revolt.

c) *Thousands of soldiers under the employment of the native states became jobless when the states were annexed to the British dominion*. As many as 60,000 families lost their livelihood, when Oudh's army was disbanded. Naturally the disbanded soldiers were seething with anger and were seeking an opportunity to strike at the new regime which had deprived them of their livelihood.

Social and religious cause

Indians had a suspicion that they would be ___converted to Christianity___ under the new regime. The fear was largely due to the activities of some of the activities of some Christian missionaries. The English also established **Chapels and Churches** for propagating Christianity at the expense of the government. Even **civil and military officers were asked to propagate the gospel**. The religious sentiments of the people were further hurt when a ___tax was imposed on the construction of temples and mosques.___

An ACT was also passed in 1856 known as the "**General Services Enlistment Act**", which imposed on the Indian sepoys the obligation to serve wherever required. This **forced Hindus for overseas travelling which was against their religious customs.**

The introduction of western innovations had unsettled the minds of the ignorant people. *The spread of English education, the construction of railways and telegraph lines, legislation for the suppression of sati and the remarriage of the widows stimulated Indians belief that the British were determined to convert the people to Christianity.* The introduction of railways was resented on the ground that people of all castes would have to travel in the same compartments. The common people did not appreciate these changes. They looked upon them as foreign innovations designed to break down the social order to which they were accustomed and which they considered sacred.

The **educated Indians were also denied high posts**. The highest office open to an Indian in Civil Services was that of a *sadar or an Amin* with an annual salary of Rs. 500 only. In the military service the highest office that an Indian could secure is that of a *Subedar*. Humiliation and **torture were inflicted upon Indians** in their own country. This racial discrimination hurt Indian sentiments tremendously.

POLITICAL CAUSES:

Lord Dalhousie's policy of annexation caused uproar among the people of India. The last Peshwa, Baji Rao's adopted son Nana Sahib was deprived of the pension his father was receiving. Rani Laxmi Bai's adopted son was not given the throne after the death of his father. The annexation of Oudh without a reason led to a huge uprising. The annexation of Jhansi, Satara and Nagpur shocked the Hindus as they were predominantly Hindu states. The remaining Hindus and Muslims who were unaffected became insecure, lest they meet the same fate.

To make matters worse Lord Dalhousie announced *in 1849 that Bahadur Shah Zafar will not be allowed to stay in the Red Fort* anymore and they were compelled to move to a place near Qutab Minar. To further worsen the situation *Lord Canning announced in 1856 that with the demise of Bahadur Shah Zafar, his successor will not be allowed to use the title "king".*

The **myth** about the superiority of the British was shattered when they were badly beaten in the first Afghan War. Besides that there was a **rumor** floated around that with the end of the Revolt of 1857 the British Raj would come to an end. This rumor created from the fact that the battle of Plassey in 1757 brought about British power and with 1857 a century would be completed which will mark the end of British rule.

MILITARY CAUSES :

The East India Company was formed with the help of Indian soldiers. Instead of giving them due credit, the Indian soldiers were made victims of suppression. Disregarding the fact that the Indian soldiers were efficient, the British officials paid them poor. Indian soldiers who had formerly held high offices in the times of the native princes found themselves in low ranks. *All the higher ranks were reserved for white men* irrespective of their capacity to perform. The futures of the soldier were doomed and bleak. There was *no hope of receiving any allowance* also. The Bengal army lacked discipline. The sepoys were unhappy as they were for the most of the times *sent overseas to fight*, which was not desirable at all. There was *no retirement age*. The bitter feeling and anger reached its highest point with the *emergence of the Enfield Rifles. The cartridges of these rifles were greased with cow and pig fats. The sepoys had to remove the cartridge with their teeth before loading them into the rifles. Both the Hindus and Muslims were discontented.* Hindus consider cow sacred and Muslims considered pigs as impure. Thus, both refused to use this cartridge and they were disharmony everywhere.

Events of WOI:

Meerut
On 6th May, 1857 A.D. 85 out of 90 Indian soldiers at Meerut refused to bite the greased cartridges with their teeth. These 85 soldiers were court-martialled and imprisoned for 10 years. They were stripped off their uniforms in the presence of the entire Indian crowd. It was too

much of a disgrace and this incident sent a wave of anger. On 10th May 1857, the Indian soldiers at Meerut broke into open revolt. They released their companions and murdered a few European officers. On the night of 10th May the mutineers marched to Delhi and reached there on 11th May.

Delhi

The revolutionaries reached from Meerut to Delhi on 11th May, 1857 and the small British garrison at Delhi was not able to resist and consequently fell into their hands within 2 days. The Mughal Emperor, Bahadur Shah Zafar, was proclaimed Emperor of India. In order to regain Delhi, Sir John Lawrence sent a strong British force commanded by John Nicholson. After a long siege of four months, the British recovered Delhi in September 1857 A.D. The Mughal Emperor Bahadur Shah Zafar was captured, his two sons and a grandson were shot dead before his eyes and he was sent to Rangoon where he died in the year 1862 A. D.

Kanpur

At Kanpur the struggle for Independence was led by Nana Sahib (The adopted son of Peshwa Baji Rao II). A number of British fell into his hands and he showed great kindness to them. But when he heard about inhuman attitude of Gen. O'Neil towards Indians, he became very furious and killed all the British. General Havelock captured Kanpur after defeating Nana Sahib in a hotly contested battle on June 17, 1857. Later on Nana Sahib, with the help of Tantya Topi, recaptured Kanpur in November, 1857 but not for a long time and British defeated them once again in a fierce war from December 1 to 6, 1857. Nana Sahib fled towards Nepal, where he probably died, while Tantya Tope migrated to Kalpi.

Lucknow

The struggle for independence at Lucknow was led by Nawab, Wajid Ali Shah. The Chief Commissioner, Sir Henry Lawrence, sought refuge with 1000 English and 700 Indian soldiers inside the Residency. The Indians did not make any concession and killed most of the Englishmen, including "ir Henry Lawrence and the notorious English General O'Neil. At last, the Commander-in-Chief General Collin Campbell marched towards Lucknow and captured it after a fierce battle in March 1858.

Jhansi   and

Gwalior: The leader of the revolutionaries in Central India was Rani Laxmi Bai of Jhansi. General Sir Huge Rose attacked Jhansi in March 1858 but the brave Rani Laxmi Bai kept the British General frightened for quite some time. She with the help of Tantya Tope created problems for the British troops. Both fought many successful battles against the British. A fierce battle was fought between the British and the revolutionaries under Rani Laxmi Bai and Tantya Tope from June 11 to June 1 8, 1 858 A. D. But the personal velour of Rani and Tantya Tope could not match the resources at the command of the British. Tantya Tope was betrayed by the Gwalior Chief Man Singh and fell into the hands of the British. He was subsequently hanged on April 18, 1859.

Reasons for the Failure of WOI:

Lack of unity amongst Indians was one of the important reasons for the failure of WOI. The war spread over a few places. Starting from Meerut it spread to Delhi, Lucknow,

Allahabad, Kanpur, Gwalior and Jhansi. Each area had its own leader. In Delhi the Mughal emperor bahadur shah II was made the commander. Hazrat mahal led the rebel forces in lucknow .Nana sahib and Tatia Topi rose up in Kanpur. Rani lakshmibai fought in Gwalior and Jhansi but there was no link and coordination between them.

The reason for lack of unity was that there was *no common cause* and no common planning. Muslims wanted to bring back Muslim rule, while Hindus wanted that the power should be in hands of Hindu rulers such as Marathas.

Another aspect of lack of unity was that there was *no common leader* and concept of nationalism was absent among Indian people. Most of the local fighters were interested in their personal security and wellbeing.

Many Indian states rulers sided and **helped the British**. Rulers of Gwalior, Kashmir, Hyderabad and Nepal were loyal and offered help to British. The **Sikh** from Punjab assisted the British to regain Delhi and the ruler of Kashmir sent 2000 troops to support the British. The leaders of Indian forces did not come to support one another.

There was also no planning, **no arrangement** for training of soldiers and no supply of weapons and funds on a regular basis which was essential to conduct a successful war. Therefore the local forces were too weak to face the British.

But besides all that the main reason for the failure of the WOI was that the British were too strong and had superiority in weapon and fighting methods. The British army was disciplined and trained. There was regular supply of weapons and funds from England. Therefore the Indian rebel forces were suppressed one by one at all the places by the British.

The war of Independence of 1857 achieved nothing.

Give reasons why you agree & disagree with this statement.

The WOI 1857 achieved nothing for Indians who were defeated and crushed by British. Delhi was captured eventually. Later Lucknow, Kanpur, Allahbad, Gawalior and Jhansi were brought under full control of British. The plan and effort of Indian rebel forces to throw the British out of India failed badly. By July 1858 all uprising was suppressed and the British had brought the whole of India under their control.

Although the Indians achieved nothing, the WOI became a source of patriotic inspiration for the Indian people during later years. The war became a symbol of people's determination to free trade from foreign rule. Educated Indians formed political parties and they adopted constitutional methods to achieve independence.

On the other hand, from the British point of view, the WOI achieved much for the British. India came directly under British government, ending the rule of EIC. The British strengthened the grip and control over India in every way. The title of governor general was changed to viceroy who was given vast powers. The British Indian Army was reorganized in such a way that in future no revolt may be possible. India became a British colony and was a source of much economic benefit. The British rule over India became a pillar of strength for the British Empire. British became the permanent power in the world. The British started building roads, railways, canals and school in India. The British gave a sound educational, judicial and administrative system to India.

EXPECTED SHORT QUESTIONS:.

Mirza Abu Zafar Sirajuddin Muhammad Bahadur Shah Zafar 24 October 1775 – 7 November 1862), also known as *Bahadur Shah Zafar* was the last Mughal emperor . He was the son of Akbar II and Lal Bai, a Hindu Rajput. He became the Mughal emperor when his father died on 28 September 1837. He used *Zafar*, a part of his name, meaning "victory" .Following his involvement in the Indian Rebellion of 1857, the British tried and then exiled him from Delhi and sent him to Rangon in British-controlled Burma. When Zafar reached the age of 87, in 1862 he was "weak and feeble". However in late October 1862, his condition deteriorated suddenly. He was "spoon-fed" but he found it difficult to do it by 3 November. Zafar finally died on Friday 7 November 1862.

Mangal Pandey 19 July 1827 – 8 April 1857), was an Indian soldier who played a key part in events immediately preceding the outbreak of the Indian rebellion of 1857.Mangal Pandey was a sepoy in the 34th Bengal Native Infantry (BNI) regiment of the British East India Company. While contemporary British opinion considered him a traitor and mutineer, Pandey is widely regarded as a freedom fighter in modern India

Suttee, the Indian custom of a widow burning herself, either on the funeral fire of her dead husband or in some other fashion, soon after his death. Although never widely practiced, suttee was the ideal of certain Brahman and royal castes. It is sometimes linked to the myth of the Hindu goddess Sati, who burned herself to death in a fire that she created through her yogic powers after her father insulted her husband, the god Shiva—but in this myth Shiva remains alive and avenges "ati's death.

Expected Questions:

Question No. 1: Briefly explain three reasons for the war of Independence of 1857.
(7)June 2000.Q.1b

Question No. 2: Was the introduction of the 'Doctrine of lapse' in 1852 the most important reasons for the war of Independence in 1857? Explain your answer. (14)June 2001 Q.1c
Question No. 3: Why did war of Independence of 1857 fail?(7)June 2002 Q,2b
Question No. 4: The war of Independence of 1857 achieved nothing .Give reasons why you agree & disagree with this statement.   (14)Nov.2002 Q.1
c

Question No. 5: The war of Independence of 1857 was caused by the Greased Cartridges incident. Give reasons why you might agree & disagree with this statement.
(14)June 2003 Q.1c
Question No. 6: A lack of unity & coordination was the main reason for the failure of the war of Independence by 1858 Do you agree?
                                                                      (14)June 2004 Q.1c

Question No 7: The introduction of Social reforms by the British, such as education, caused the war of Independence in 187.' Do you agree? Give reasons for your answer.

Question No. 8: "The establishment of English as the official language of the sub continent in 1834 was the main reason for the war of Independence of1857' .Do you agree or disagree? Give reasons for your answer.
(14)June2007Q.2c

Question No. 9: Why did the war of Independence of1857 fail?

(7)Nov.2007Q.2b

Question No. 10: Religious factors were more important than any other in causing the war of independence of 1857-58. Do you agree? Give reasons for your answer.

(14)Nov.2008 Q.1 c

Question No. 11: explain the three reasons for the failure of the war of Independence 1857-1858.
(7) Nov 2009.Q.1 b

Question No. 12: was a lack of unity amongst the Indians the main reasons for the failure of the war of Independence 1857-58? Explain your answer. (14)June2010Q.1c

Question No. 13: in 1857,a number of sepoys refused to use the new cartridges at Meerut ,near Delhi. The sepoys were given long prison sentences and this led to a revolt in which their fellow sepoys marched on Delhi and massacred all the British they could find. Things got worse for the British at Kanpur.
   (a)   What happened at the battle of Kanpur? (4)June2011Q.2a

Question No.14: Did educational reforms have a more important effect on the Indians than the social, religious and economic ones introduced by the British during the years 1773 to 1856? Explain your answer.   (14)   Nov.2011 Q.1c

Question No.15: was the greased cartridges incident the most important cause of the war of independence of 1857? Explain your answer. (14)June2012Q.1c

Question No.16:

Read the source below carefully to answer question (a).
Indians began to resent British control of the sub-continent, and in 1857 the British faced a serious challenge to their control of India. For the British it was a revolt against their authority but for the Indians it was a revolt to throw off foreign domination.
(a) Describe the events of the War of Independence, 1857–1858. (4)June2013Q.2a

Question No.17: Why did the War of Independence fail to meet its aims in 1857? (7)Nov.2013Q.2b

Question No.18: "The strength of the British army was the sole reason for the failure of the War of Independence by 1858." Do you agree? Give reasons for your answer. (14)Nov.2014Q.1c

SIR SYED AHMED KHAN 1817-1898:

Early Biographical details:

- **Born in 1817** in Delhi.
- By the age of 18 he was skilled in Arabic, Persian, Mathematics and Medicine.
- In 1838 his father died and he was forced to seek an employment and became the judge in Delhi in 1846.
- This year (1846) he wrote his book on Archeology called ***Athas-al-Sanadeed***.
- In the war of Independence 1857 he was working as a chief Judge in Bijnaur & saved lives of many English women & children.
- As a reward of his loyalty, British offered him a state with a large income but he refused.
- Later he was appointed Chief Justice in Muradabad and then transferred to Ghazipure.
- In 1864 he was transferred to **Aligarh** where he worked to establish a new college.
- **Aligarh** became the Centre of a **'Muslim ꞌenaissance'.**
- He died on 27th March **1898**.

Beliefs:

Sir Syed was extremely unhappy about the position of Muslims in the subcontinent. Since the days of the Mughal declined the social and economic status of Muslims had declined sharply and the role of Muslims in the war of Independence had left further decline as British took measures to ensure that their control was unchallenged.
Sir Syed Ahmed felt that the poor status of Muslims was due to they were treated as second- class citizen by British and Hindus and they had to take some responsibilities themselves. Most Muslims thought that British were no more than just invaders and they had nothing to do with them. Sir Syed Ahmed believed that Muslims had to accept that the British were there rulers and could only improve if they have a positive approach towards them. They needed to accept the British idea and their education if they wanted to improve. Sir Syed wanted to see Muslims untied and prospering in their social, economic and religious fortune. He made this his Life's ambition and founded Aligarh movement to create educational and political awareness among Muslims of India.

Educational Reforms/Aligarh College:

Sir Syed's greatest achievement was his ***Aligarh Movement***, which was primarily an educational venture. He established ***Gulshan School at Muradabad in 1859, Victoria School at Ghazipur in 1863, and a scientific society in 1864***. When Sir Syed was posted at Aligarh in 1867, he started the ***Muhammadan Anglo-Oriental School*** in the city. Sir Syed got the opportunity to visit

England in 1869-70. During his stay, he studied the British educational system and appreciated it. On his return home he decided to make **M. A. O. High School** on the pattern of British boarding schools. The School later became a college in 1875. The status of University was given to the college after the death of Sir Syed in 1920. M. A. O. High School, College and University played a big role in the awareness of the Muslims of South Asia.

A brief chronology of Syed Ahmad's efforts is given below:

1859: Built **Gulshan School in Muradabad**.

1863: Set up **Victoria School in Ghazipur.**

1864: Set up the **Scientific Society in Aligarh.** This society was involved in the translation of English works into the native language.

1866: Aligarh Institute Gazette. This imparted information on history; ancient and modern science of agriculture, natural and physical sciences and advanced mathematics.

1870: Committee Striving for the Educational Progress of Muslims.

1875: Muhammadan Anglo-Oriental School (M. A. O.), Aligarh, set up on the pattern of English public schools. Later rose to the level of college in 1877 and university in 1920.

1886: Muhammadan Educational Conference. This conference met every year to take stock of the educational problems of the Muslims and to persuade them to get modern education and abstain from politics. It later became the political mouthpiece of the Indian Muslims and was the forerunner of the Muslim League.

Syed Ahmad Khan's Aligarh Movement played a significant role in bringing about an intellectual revolution among the Indian Muslims. Thus it succeeded in achieving its major objectives, i.e. educational progress and social reform. His efforts earned Sir Syed the title "**Prophet of Education".**

"Sir Saiyad was a prophet of education " (Mahatma Gandhi)

"The real greatness of the man (Sir Saiyad) consists in the fact that he was the first Indian Muslim who felt the need of a fresh orientation of Islam and worked for it" (Sir Allama Iqbal)

Reconciliation Policy:

Unlike other Muslim leaders of his time, Sir Syed was of the view that Muslims should have friendship with the British if they want to take their due rights. To achieve this he did a lot to convince the British that Muslims were not against them. On the other hand, he tried his best to convince the Muslims that if they did not befriend the British, they could not achieve their goals. Sir Syed wrote many books and journals to remove the misunderstandings between Muslims and the British. The most significant of his literary works were his pamphlets **"Loyal Muhammadans of India" and "Cause of Indian Revolt"**. He also wrote **a commentary on the Bible,** in which he attempted to prove that Islam is the closest religion to Christianity. ***Tabyin-ul- Kalam and "A Series of Essays on the Life of Muhammad*** helped to create cordial relations between the British Government and the Indian Muslims. They also helped to remove misunderstandings about Islam and Christianity.

Political Reforms:

Sir Syed asked the Muslims of his time not to participate in politics unless and until they got modern education. He was of the view that Muslims could not succeed in the field of western politics without knowing the system. He was invited to attend the first session of the Indian **National Congress** and to join the organization but he refused to accept the offer. He also asked the Muslims to keep themselves away from the Congress and predicted that the party would prove to be a pure Hindu party in the times to come. By establishing the **Muhammadan Educational Conference,** he provided Muslims with a platform on which he could discuss their political problems. It was from this platform that Syed Ahmad Khan strongly advised the Muslims against joining the Hindu dominated Congress. He was in favor ***of reserved seats*** for Muslims and also promoted the idea that Hindus and Muslims are two distinct nations. This idea led to the **Two-Nation Theory.**

URDU HINDI CONTROVERSY 1867:

During the last days of the Muslim rule, Urdu emerged as the most common language of the northwestern provinces of India. It was declared the official language, and all official records were written in this language. In 1867, some prominent Hindus started a movement in Banaras in which they demanded the replacement of Urdu with Hindi, and the Persian script with the **Deva Nagri** script, as the court language in the northwestern provinces. The reason for opposing Urdu was that the language was written in Persian script, which was similar to the Arabic script and Arabic, was the language of the Quran, the Holy Book of the Muslims. The movement grew quickly and within a few months spread throughout the Hindu population of the northwestern provinces of India. The headquarters of this movement were in Allahabad.

This situation provoked the Muslims to come out in order to protect the importance of the Urdu language. The opposition by the Hindus towards the Urdu language made it clear to the Muslims of the region that Hindus were not ready to tolerate the culture and traditions of the Muslims.

The Urdu-Hindi controversy had a great effect on the life of Sir Syed Ahmad Khan. Before this event he had been a great advocate of Hindu-Muslim unity and was of the opinion that the ***"two nations are like two eyes of the beautiful bride, India"***. But this movement completely altered his point of view. He put forward the ***Two-Nation Theory***, predicting that the differences between the two groups would increase with the passage of time and the two communities would not join together in anything wholeheartedly. Sir Syed was the first person who used the words ***"My Nation"*** for Muslims and the words "Two Nation" in the subcontinent .His main idea was the protection and the safeguard of rights of Muslims in the sub-continent.

Expected Questions and Answers:

Question No. 1: Were the educational developments the most important contribution of Sir Syed Ahmed Khan in his attempt to improve the relations between the Muslims and the British? Explain your answer.   14
June 2000 Q.1 (c)

Question No.2: Why did Sir Syed Ahmed Khan try to improve relations between the Muslims and the British?   7
November 2000 Q.2 (b)

Question No.3: Why did Sir Syed Ahmed Khan develop his *Two Nation Theory*?   7
June 2001, Q.2 (b)

Question No.4: Was the attempt to achieve a better understanding with the British the most important contribution that Sir Syed Ahmed Khan made to the Muslim cause during the 19th century? Explain your answer.   14
June 2005 Q.1 (c)

Question No.5: "ir "yed Ahmed Khan's political beliefs had a greater impact on the Muslims than any of his other beliefs. Do you agree or disagree? Give reason for your answer.
     1

4
November 2007. Q.2 (c)

Question No.6: Why did Sir Syed wish to develop a better understanding with the British following the War of Independence (1857-58)? 7
June 2008 Q.2 (b)

Question No.7: was the development of a western education system the most important contribution of Sir Syed Ahmed Khan in developing the cause of Muslims during the 19th century? Explain your answer. 1June 2009 Q.2 (c)

Question No.8: was the religious view of Sir Syed his most important contribution in developing the cause of Muslims during 19th century? Explain your answer. 14 November 2010.

Q.3(c)**Question No.9:** Why did Sir Syed found Aligarh Movement? 7 June 2011 Q.2 (b)

Question No.10: Sir Syed Ahmad Khan admired many British ways of doing things. At the same time he had a great faith in the Muslim religion. He was convinced that if the British ever left

India the Muslims would be dominated by the overwhelming Hindu majority. He decided to do something about this. He published a pamphlet called 'The Loyal Mohammedans of India.'
(a) What was 'The Loyal Mohammedans of India'?
November 2011 Q.2 (a)   4

Question No.11: Read the source below carefully to answer question (a).
Sir Syed Ahmad Khan was determined to improve the status of Muslims. He had a desire to re- establish good relations with the British which, he hoped, would lead to greater opportunities for Muslims. He also believed that Muslims should have good relations with Hindus. However, he was concerned about the 'Hindu-Urdu Controversy.'
(a) Describe the 'Hindu-Urdu Controversy. 'November 2012 Q.14

Question No.12: Was the Two Nation Theory the most important contribution of Sir Syed Ahmad Khan? Explain your answer.
June 2013 Q.2(c)14

Question No.13: Read the source below carefully to answer question (a).
Sir Syed Ahmad Khan decided to change Muslim attitudes towards receiving British education. He travelled to England to study the university system there. He believed in setting up a university for Muslims in the sub-continent and was impressed by the universities of Oxford and Cambridge. However, on his return home he found that his plans were met with suspicion from some people. Nevertheless he wanted to pursue the idea of providing better education for Muslims.
(a) What was the Mohammedan Anglo-Oriental School?4 November 2013 Q.2 (a)

Question No. 14: Why did Sir Syed Ahmad Khan try to improve relations between the Muslims and the British?
Oct Nov 2014 Q.1(b)   7

Answer to Question No. 5:

Sir Syed Ahmed Khan's political beliefs had a great impact on Muslims. This service of Sir Syed aimed at restoring the prestige, social position, political importance & economic well-being of Muslims. In the beginning Sir Syed believed that all people living in India (Hindus & Muslims) were one nation. But the Hindi – Urdu controversy convinced him that the two communities would not pull on together under one government peacefully. Thus he changed his political belief to Two Nation Theory .This theory later became the basis of creation of Pakistan. Sir Syeds other important political services include his advice to Muslim not to join the congress. He realized that Muslim minority will always be dominated by Hindu majority under the modern democratic system which the congress was demanding at that time & the British were trying to introduce in India. Therefore he suggested to the British government that some arrangement should be made to ensure Muslim representation in all assemblies. This later resulted in the rule of separate electorate for Muslims which was introduced in 1909 reforms.

Congress also suggested that appointment in the government services should be made through competitive examinations. In this Muslims had no chance because they lagged behind the Hindus in education. Sir Syed suggested to the government that Muslims should be given jobs according to their ratio in population till they reach the same educational standard as the Hindus. Thus Sir Syed's political beliefs had a profound impact on Muslims.

But Sir Syed's services in other sectors were not less important. In fact Sir Syed gave so much importance to modern education that his efforts & contribution to Muslim education is considered to be the most important service for the betterment of Muslims of India. He established Scientific Society & published Aligarh Institute Gazette in order to introduce modern scientific developments to the Muslims. He visited England in 1869 on his own expenses to study the British educational system and to observe the working of British universities. His most important contribution in education sector was the founding of MAO College at Aligarh in 1877. Later he founded the Mohammedan Educational Conference .Its objective was to discuss and solve the educational problems of Muslims in the Sub-Continent. His effort for the cause of Muslim education served double purpose. It helped the Muslims in their economic well-being & raised status in society. It also helped in removing the mistrust between the British & the Muslims. In this way education was the most important aspect of all of "Sir Syed's services for the Muslims of India.

Another service of sir Syed after 1857 was the removal of misunderstanding between the British and the Muslims. He came to the conclusion that Muslims were being handicapped because of the misunderstanding & lack of trust between them (Muslim) & the British. The Muslims thought that the British had taken over the rule of India from Muslim rulers. Therefore the Muslims opposed & hated everything associated with the British. The Muslims kept away from English & modern education which the British were introducing in India on the other hand the British held the Muslims responsible for the uprising of 1857 & considered them (Muslims) to be their enemies. The result of this misunderstanding was that Muslims were being crushed in every way.
Therefore Sir Syed's foremost task was to remove the misunderstanding by addressing both the British and the Muslims. Sir Syed wrote books and explained to the British that the real cause of the events of 1857 was the wrong policies & attitude of the British themselves .To Muslims Sir Syed explained that Christianity & Christians should not be hated. He specially stressed that Islam does not stop them from learning modern sciences & English language. He clearly emphasized that Muslims should come towards modern education, the lack of which was causing continual set back to the Muslims of India.

Therefore it can be said that Sir Syed's political beliefs had a great impact on Muslims, but his other services especially in the field of education were more important.

Topic: 8 LANGUAES

URDU

Urdu is the national language of Pakistan since 1947. The main differences between the urdu and Hindustani is that Urdu is conventionally written in **Nastaliq calligraphy** style while Hindi is conventionally written in **Devanāgarī**.

Urdu is the national language of Pakistan and is spoken and understood throughout the country, where it shares official language status with English. It is used in education, literature, and office and court business.

The word *Urdu* itself comes from a Turkic word *ordu,* "tent" or "army," from which English also gets the word "horde." Hence Urdu is sometimes called "**Lashkarī zabān**" or "the language of the army." Furthermore, armies of India were often composed of soldiers with various native tongues. Hence, Urdu was the language chosen to address the soldiers, as it abridged several languages.

In 1947, Urdu was established as the national language of Pakistan, in the hope that this move would unite and homogenize the various ethnic groups of the new nation. Urdu suddenly went from the language of a minority to the language of the majority. Today, Urdu is taught throughout Pakistani schools and spoken in government positions.

Key Points:
- It is a mixture of *Turkish, Persian, Punjabi* & other languages.
- *Amir Khusrau* (1253-1325) had a prominent position in its development.
- It was used in the Mughal period dates back as far as the era of the sultans of Delhi.

- Urdu was decided to be the **national language of Pakistan** as it was the **symbol of unity** between the different regions of the new country.
- Urdu was chosen because of **rich literally & poetry** background which helped to promote its use.
- The language received a boost when Emperor Muhammad Shah & Bahdur Shah Zafar took an interest in promoting it. Famous poets are Mir, Sauda, Dard & Ghalib.
- **Ali Garh Muslim University** also became a center for the study of Urdu & produced talented writers like Hasrat Mohani,Majaz & jazbi.
- In the early 20th century Dr. *Allama Iqbal , Dr. Nazir Ahmed, Mohammad Husain Azad, Maulana Altaf Husain Hali & Allama Shibli* greatly enriched Urdu prose.

- Its link to the Islamic religion has also been very important, most notably with the ***translation of the Holy Quran*** by Shah Abdul Qadir.

- In the 20th century Urdu ***played a major role in struggle* for *independence***.
- British made English the official language but some of its educational institutes like ***Fort William College*** took interest in Urdu & promoted it.
- Quaide-e-Azam was keen to promote Urdu as he saw it as a ***unifying force in the country & linking language for all the provinces of thecountry.***

- Urdu set as the medium of radio & television besides medium of instruction in many schools of Pakistan.
- Urdu Plays & films were prepared & became popular soon. Urdu novels, poetry, magazines & newspapers were written which were liked by the people & widely read.
- The government of Pakistan took different steps for the promotion of Urdu.

  (i) ***Anjuman-e-Taraqia urdu & Akadmy Adbiatt Pakistan***
  (ii) As national language in the constitution of 1956, 1962, 1973.
  (iii) Urdu teaching & research at M.A, M.Phil & PhD levels.
  (iv) NIC in Urdu.
  (v) Promotion through Electronic & Print Media.

SINDHI

Sindhi is the language of the Sindh region. It is the third most spoken language of Pakistan, and the official language of Sindh in Pakistan, The government of Pakistan issues ***national identity cards*** to its citizens only in two languages, Sindhi and Urdu. Its main influence was thus a local version of spoken form of Sanskrit.

Sindhi is taught as a first language in the schools of Sindh and as a second language in Balochistan in Pakistan. Sindhi has a vast vocabulary and a very old literary tradition. This trend has made it a favourite of many writers and consequently a vast volume of literature and poetry have been written in Sindhi.

Key Points:

- Compared with Urdu, Sindhi is an old language which is being spoken in the province of Sindh.
- Documents show that as far as the 12th century it was spoken in the same form as it is today.
- Before the arrival of Muslims, Sindhi was written in 'Marwari' & ARZ Nagari ways of language.
- Sindhi has been influenced by the both Arabic & the languages brought by the Turkish tribes & Persians.
- The most famous poets of Sindhi are *Makhdum Nuh of Hala* & *Qazi Qazan* of Thatta.

- Sindhi literature was on its peak during the *somrroo* period among 1050- 1300& from 1685-1783.
- The poetry of *Sachal Sarmast* & *Shah Abdul Latif Bhattai* is particularly famous for spread of Islam, Humanity & peace.

- In **1948, Sindhi Literary Board** was set up & authors like Pir Ali Muhammad Rashdi,Faqir Nabi Bux & G.Alllana wrote many books to promote the language.
- In 1954, *Bazm-e-Talib-ul-Maula* was set up to promote its literature.
- A **'Sarmast' academy** was established in the memory of sachal Sarmast.
- A *Sindhiology department* was established at Sindh University jamshoru.
- Several newspapers published in Sindhi, such as **Ibrat, Naw-i-Sind** and **Khadim-I-Watan** besides a number of Weeklies.

PASHTTO

Pashto also known as **Afghani,** and *Pathani* ,In Pakistan, Pashto is spoken in the provinces of the Khyber Pakhtunkhwa, FATA, and Balochistan, as well as parts of Mianwali and Attock districts of Punjab province. Modern Pashto-speaking communities are also found in the cities of Karachi and Hyderabad in Sindh. With close to 7 million ethnic Pashtuns by some estimates, Karachi hosts one of the largest Pashtun populations in the world.

Key points:

- Pashto is the language spoken by the people of KPK & in the northern area of Pakistan.
- It is influenced by Arabic, Persian & Greek.
- The history of Pashto literature can be divided into three periods.
  - (i) first one starts from 2nd to the e13th century & its first poet was Ami khan Pehivan but the most famous was *Bayazid Ansari* who wrote first book on Sufism, 'khair-ul-Bian'.
  - (ii) The second begins from the Muslim invasions on India in the early 13th century & lasted for 100 years & in this period its quality was on the peak. In this age the well-known literally personalities were Sadat Ali Khan, Amir Mohammad Ansari & Hazra Mian Umer.
  - *(iii)* The third period extends to the establishment of British rule & it was also a golden age for Pashto literature as high quality writing was produced. Famous writers of this age are Arkhund Dardeeza & **Khushal Khan Khttak** & Sufi poet *Rehman Babba*.

- Sahibzada Abdul Qayum worked tirelessly to increase the political awareness in the people of NWFP & because of his efforts **Islamia College** was set up in Peshawar where Pashto was taught & soon it became the centre of freedom.
- Within three years of independence, Peshawar University was established where Pashto is taught up to Post Graduate level.
- An *academy* for the promotion of Pashto was set up in 1954 & it was initially headed by Maulana Abdul Qadir.This academy prepared a dictionary of Pashto language which is widely accepted.

PUNJABI

Punjabi is the mother tongue of the majority of people in Pakistan. According to last census 60.43 per cent Pakistanis spoke punjabi, followed by Pushto for 13.14 per cent, Sindhi for 11.77 per cent, Urdu for 7.60 per cent and Baluchi for 3.02 per cent. The rich tradition of Punjabi literature, going back to the 12th century AD when Baba Farid composed his poetry in a highly developed and sophisticated Punjabi language.

Key points:

- Punjabi is the language spoken in the most populous of Pakistan's province, the Punjab but also in other areas like Azad Kashmir & NWFP.
- It is an easily understood language & it has been given various names throughout the history such as 'Masoode', Al-Hindi & Hindko.
- It is thought that in **1080** *Hafiz Barkurdar* was the first person to have used the term 'Punjabi' to describe the language.
- Punjabi has a long history .first it was written in *Gurmukhi* Script but during the latter years of the Mughals, Arabic script was used.
- Punjabi has been influenced by many other languages such as Sindhi, Pashto, Persian, Arabic, Hindi, and Turkish & English.
- The early Punjabi literature consists of folk tales among them are *Heer Ranjha,Sassi-Pannu,Sohni Mahiwal* are widely known.
- Sufii poets such as *Baba Farid Ganjshakar,Sultan Baho* wrote their famous works in Punjabi.
- Bullhe shah composed mystical & melodious Kafis which are commonly sung these days.

- At the beginning of 20th century novels, short stories & dramas were published in Punjabi but later books on academic subjects like Law, Medicine, and History & Philosophy have also been published in the language.
- Punjabi poetry is famous & it brought new mediums, ghazal & nazam.
- **Quran** has also been translated in this language by Mohammad Ali Faiq.
- **Ustad Damman,Sharif Kunjahi,Ahmed Rahi & Munir Niazi** are the major exponents of the new wave of Punjabi.
- Punjabi literature is now taught up to MA level at the **University of Punjab.**
- The **radio, television & the film** have provided immense impetus to the recent Punjabi writing.
- Punjabi films have gained unprecedented popularity. Punjabi theatre is also very famous.

BALOCHI

- Balochi is spoken in the largest province of Pakistan, Balochistan.
- There are two main kinds of Balochi languages, Sulemanki & Mekrani.
- Balochi was brought here by nomadic tribes of North West Iran. As it was brought by nomad people, there is not enough development in this language.
- Jam Darang is considered an important Balochi poet.
- Balochi language was first time known outside the region when British traveler W.Leech reported in the 'Journal of Asiatic Society' about it.
- Before partition Balochi literature was beginning to decline but after partition steps were taken to promote it.

- *Radio Pakistan Karachi* began broadcasts in Balochi.
- Famous **B**alochi poets are Atta Shad & Ishaq Shamin.
- Famous writers are Gul Khan Nazir & Azad Jamal Din.
- *Quetta University* offers Master's degree in Balochi.
- The **Balochi literary Association** was set up which published many magazines and articles in Balochi language.
- A weekly magazine known as **"Nan Kessan"** was published. A monthly known as **"Olassis"** was also published.
- Translation of the Bible has also been published in Balochi language.

PASTPAPERS QUESTIONS:

Question No.1: How successful has Pakistan been in promoting its regional languages? Explain your answer.
14 Nov. 2000, Q.2 c

Question No. 2: Why did Pakistan choose Urdu as its national language? 7Nov. 2001 Q.1 b

Question No. 3: how successful has been the promotion of the following regional languages in Pakistan between 1947 & 1988.

        (I)   Punjabi
        (II)   Pushto
        (III)   Sindhi?

Explain your answer with reference to all three of the languages.14 June 2002, Q.2 c

Question No. 4: The development of Pushto has been promoted more than any other Pakistani regional language between 1947 & 1988. Give reasons why you might agree & disagree with this statement.14 Nov. 2003. Q.3 c

Question No.5: Why was Urdu chosen as the national language of Pakistan? 7 June 2004, Q. 4 b

Question   No. 6: How important was the development of regional languages to Pakistan between 1947 & 1980? Explain your answer.
14 Nov. 2004, Q.3 c

Question No.7: Why did Pakistan choose Urdu as its national language? 7Nov. 2005, Q.2 b

Question No.8: The promotion of regional languages in Pakistan between 1947 & 1988 has been more successful than the promotion of Urdu. Do you agree, explain your answer. 14 June 2006, Q.1c

Question No.9: Sindhi was promoted more than other regional language between 1947 & 1988. Do you agree or disagree? Give reasons for your answer. 14Nov.2007 Q.1 c

Question No.10: has the promotion of Urdu been more successful than that of any regional language in Pakistan between 1947 and 1988? Explain your answer.
14 June 2009, Q.1 c

Question No.11: why have regional languages been promoted by the Pakistani government since 1947? 7 Nov.2009 Q.2 b
Question No.12: how has the government promoted the development of Balochi since 1947?
4 Nov.2010 Q.2 a
Question No.13: Punjabi has been promoted more than other regional language between 1947 & 1999. Do you agree or disagree? Give reasons for your answer. 14 june2011 Q.2 c

Question No.14: Explain the choice of Urdu in 1947 as the national language of Pakistan. 7 Nov.2011 Q.1 b

Question No.15: Language is extremely important in the development of any nation. A common language helps to build a shared understanding of what a nation believes in. Urdu became the national language of Pakistan but, due to the diversity of languages and culture across the country, many regional languages have been promoted by the government. One of these is Punjabi.

How has the Pakistan government promoted the development of Punjabi? 4 Nov. 2012 Q.2 a

Question No.16: Why have regional languages been promoted by the Pakistan government since 1947? June 2013 Q.1 b

Question No.17: 1 Read the source below carefully to answer question (a).
After Independence, Urdu became the national language as it was a unifying force in the new country. It was seen as the link language for all the provinces to provide for the cultural and educational needs of the people. However, it was also recognised that regional languages had an important role to play in the newly formed country. One of these was Sindhi.
(a) How has Pakistan promoted the development of Sindhi since 1947? Nov. 2013 Q 1.c

ANSWER TO QUESTION NO. 16:

- Regional languages were promoted because they were spoken by a large number of people. Government also believed that the promotion will be helpful in national unity and integrity because promotion of language and culture gives a sense of pride among people.
- Punjabi, Sindhi and Pashto have a vast literature and had an important role in independence movement and creation of Pakistan. So it was necessary to promote these languages.
- Balochi language had little development before 1947 and its literature was in decline. Therefore Balochi was promoted to bring it in line with other regional languages.
- Urdu was declared as the national language. Promotion of regional language was necessary so that people of different provinces may not feel that Urdu was being imposed on them and their own language was being ignored.
- It was also felt that the literature and work undertaken by authors in such areas as Sindh should be kept alive and so the government set up bodies to promote it such as the Sindhi Literary Board in 1948.
- Many languages have played an important role in the history of the region, eg Pushto literature had an important role in creating opposition to British rule and the movement for independence.

TOPIC 9:

Partition of Bengal and Reversal 1905-11

Introduction

The partition of Bengal was the most important event during the rule of Lord Curzon. It was carried out mainly for the convenience of administration. Bengal in those days was the biggest province of India extending over 1, 89, 000 square miles with a population of 80 million. It was comprising of Bengal, Behar and Orissa and was under the central of one lieutenant Governor. After Lord Curzon took charge as Governor General of India the discussion over the Partition began due to the following issues:

Reasons for partition of Bengal

1.   **Vastness of Province:** The Province was spread over the area of 1, 89, 000 square miles with the population of 80 million, which was too vast to be managed by one lieutenant Governor. He could not make a tour for the whole province due to its vastness once in his tenure.

2.   **Limited Sources of Communication:** The sources of communication in the provinces were limited due to rivers and forests. The law and order condition of the provinces was also worst due to insufficient police and in-efficient management. Therefore the need of partition of province was felt severally.

3.   **Difference of Language:** There was also the difference of Languages and civilization of the natives of West Bengal and East Bengal. The natives of West Bengal considered themselves superior in civilization to the resident of East Bengal. The Condition demanded for the division of Provinces.

4.   **Promotion of Trade:** The division of Bengal was the need of the time to develop trade in East Bengal and to promote the Port of Chittagong, which could be done only by division of the Provinces.

5: **Appeasement policy**: It is also believed that the British wanted to **appease Muslims** and certainly the partition went in favour of the Muslims. Before the partition only Western Bengal was developed and industrialized. It was a striking contrast to the eastern part where the Muslim peasantry was crushed under the Hindu landlords, the river system was infested with pirates, and very few funds were allocated for education. The partition helped boost Bengali literature and language; efforts were also made towards the social, economic and educational uplift of the Muslims.

6: Divide and rule policy: Bengali Hindus also alleged that Lord Curzon had deliberately tried to **divide the Hindus** and the Muslims by drawing a line between the Hindu and the Muslim halves of Bengal. And by favouring the Muslims by giving them a new province in which they were in a clear majority, had struck a deadly blow to Bengali nationality. They branded him as the upholder of the devilish policy of _'**divide and rule'**._

7. Partition: The Partition of Bengal was thus calculated to restore efficiency in the Government and administration on one hand and encouraged local initiatives for progress and development on the other. Lord Curzon partitioned Bengal and formed two new provinces of manageable size – East and West Bengal. East Bengal consisted of Dacca, Mamansingh, Assam, Kaula, Rangpur, and Bogra district, the Dacca was capital of East Bengal constituted a majority Muslim Province, while the Bihar and Orissa constituted a separate province to be called as West Bengal with the capital of Calcutta and become the Hindu Majority provinces.

East Bengal contained a population of **eighteen million Muslims** and twelve million Hindus. Whereas West Bengal had a population fifty four million of which 42 million where Hindus and thus was the Hindu majority province.

Muslims' Response

It received a favourable response from the Muslims. It was thought that it would bring the emancipation of Muslims socially and economically. The Muslims welcomed the Partition of Bengal for the following reasons:

1.   In the majority province of East Bengal the Muslims would be free from Hindu dominance in economic field. They would get opportunities of services and advancement of agriculture.

2.   The city of Dacca, where the Muslims were in majority was the centre of Muslim culture. In Dacca Muslims had a great chance of success for social and cultural advancement than in Calcutta.

3.   The Partition could result in political uplift and securing represent action in the Government.

4.   The partition of Bengal relieved the Muslims from competing with Hindus, who were more advanced in every field of life.

Hindus Response

The Hindus did not accept it, as it dealt a telling blow to their monopolies and exclusive hold on economic, social, Political life of the whole of Bengal. They called it as a deliberate attempt by British Government

1. The Partition of Bengal had brightened the possibility of betterment of Muslims; while the Hindu landlords, capitalists and traders wanted status quo and to continue the exploitation of the Muslims.

2. Hindu lawyers also reacted to the partition of Bengal because they thought that the new province would have its separate courts and thus their practice would be affected.

3. Hindu press was not different from that of Hindu advocates. Hindus had their monopoly over almost whole of the province press. They were afraid that new newspapers would be established which would decrease their income naturally.

4. The Hindus launched **Swadeshi** Movement whose sole purpose was to boycott of British goods.

5. Murder attempts also began. Not only Lord Minto but many other British officials and Muslim leaders were attacked by Hindu extremist.

Annulment of the Partition

When Lord Harding assumed charge as Governor General of India Hindus again became active and sent a representation to him for the annulment of partition of Bengal. He recommended the same to the British Prime Minister for Indian Affairs. On the occasion of the visiting His Majesty George V to Indo-Pakistan and holding of Darbar at Delhi on 12th December 1911 the partition of Bengal was cancelled.

The united Bengal was placed under a Governor and Assam was placed under a Chief Commissioner. This decision was shattering blow to Muslims. It left them disillusioned. Their anger and indignation had widespread repercussions. The Muslims leaders and intelligentsia condemned the decision as betrayal of worst kind.

Expected Question & Answers:

Question No. 1: why was the partition of Bengal reversed in 1911? (7) June 2001. Q. 3 b

Question No.2: how did the Hindus oppose the partition of Bengal between 1905 & 1911? (7) November 2002 Q. 2 b

Question No. 3: why was the partition of Bengal reversed in 1911? (7) November 2003 Q.2b

Question no.4: why was Bengal partitioned in 1905? (7) June 2004 Q.2b

Question No.5: why was the partition of Bengal reversed in 1911? (7) November 2005 Q. 3 b

Question No. 6: Bengal was partitioned in 1905 because of geographical factors. Do you agree? Explain your answer. (14)June 2006 Q.2c

Question No.7: why did the British decide to reverse the partition of Bengal in 1911?(7) June 2007 Q. 2 b

Question No.8: the reasons for partitioning Bengal in 1905 were more important than those that caused its reversal in 1911, do you agree? Explain your answer.(14) June 2009 Q.3c

Question No.9: partition or reversal? Were the reasons why Bengal was partitioned in 1905 more important than those regarding its reversal in 1911? Explain your answer.(14) June 2011 Q.3c

Question no.10: why was Bengal partitioned in 1905? (7) Oct/Nov 2012 Q.2b

Question N.o.11: Bengal was the largest province of India with a population of 85 million people. Lord Curzon, the newly appointed Viceroy believed that Bengal was too large to be governed efficiently as a single province and in 1903 proposed that it should be split into two, West Bengal and East Bengal. Describe the Swadeshi Movement   [4]Oct/Nov 2014 Q. 2a

Answer to Question No. 2:

The Hindu community from all over India strongly opposed it. They launched a mass movement, declaring October 16 as a *day of mourning* in Calcutta. Influenced by the Chinese boycott of American goods, the Hindus started the **Swadeshi Movement** against the British. In the meantime, the Hindus raised the Band-i-Mataram as the national cry protecting worship of Shivaji as a national hero. This organized anarchist movement took a terrorist turn resulting in political sabotage and communal riots.

The Partition movement was also strongly opposed from the beginning by the Bengali Hindu middle-class, who felt it was a deliberate blow by the British against the solidarity of the Bengali-speaking population. They believed the British government was fostering a strong Muslim nation in order to keep within check the rapidly growing Hindu power in the West.

This period saw the growth of the Indian National Congress, who condemned the Partition and considered it an attempt at British 'divide and rule'. The Congress grew from a middle-class pressure group to become the main platform for a nation-wide nationalist movement centered on the goals of **Swaraj** (self-government) and **Swadeshi** (boycotting the import of British manufactured goods).

British reacted sharply. Restrictions were made on newspaper & public meetings. Between 1906 & 1908 the editors were prosecuted & imprisoned. In June 1908, Tilak was arrested & was put into prison for 6 years. Other leaders left India to avoid arrest. The British decided to win the support of the Hindus by making reforms, Known as Morley Minto reforms. But it was too late. British government decided to change of their strategy because of murder attempts and economic disaster. Partition of Bengal was reversed in 1911. Lord Harding, new Viceroy agreed to reverse partition. Announcement at Durbar in Delhi on 12 December by King George British decided to reverse the partition because they were forced to do so. British also moved the capital from Calcutta to Delhi.

Answer to Question No. 6:

Bengal had been one of the most important provinces of the sub-continent due to its best agriculture. British government spent a lot of power and money to administrate Bengal but ultimately they decided to divide it in 1903. Apparently it is believed that Bengal was divided due to its geographical factor and to some extent it is correct. Indeed Bengal was the biggest province and it was very hard to keep an eye on the dense jungles, deep marshy areas and extremely populated regions of Bengal. Its population expanded to 95 million which was ten times greater than the population of Britain at that time.

It was difficult to govern & effectively administer such a large province & the idea of partitioning it was brewing in the minds of the Britain rulers for quite some time. Lord Curzon gave a serious thought to it & got the approval of the British government. Bengal was partitioned into two provinces in October 1905 & provinces of West Bengal & East Bengal & Assam were created. The division of Dacca, Chittagong, MymenSingh were annexed to Assam. After the partition was enforced, it transpired that west Bengal had a Hindu majority population, while East Bengal & Assam had a Muslim majority population. The emergence of a Muslim majority province pleased the Muslim because it gave a chance for progress of the Muslim community in fields of education, jobs in government services & commerce. Under United Bengal, the province was dominated by Hindus who were better educated, economically better off & more well-organized, while Muslims lagged behind in every field.

The Hindus of Bengal bitterly opposed the partition & blamed the British that the partition had been enforced with sinister motives. In fact the Hindu businessmen of Calcutta feared a reduction in their income & profits. Therefore they started mass agitation against the partition of Bengal & their protest was supported by the congress. Muslims were disorganized & were unable to counter the congress & Hindu propaganda.

In fact, partition of Bengal was done not to favour or harm any community. The partition was done mainly because of geographical ground realities.

Topic 10

SIMLA DEPUTATION AND MUSLIM LEAGUE 1906:

What was   the   Simla   Deputation?

The Simla Deputation of 1906 was the first systematic attempt on the part of the Muslims to present their demands, to the British government and to seek their acceptance. The Simla deputation comprised **35 Muslims** from all over India. It was a galaxy of Muslims leaders from all the provinces, from one end of India to the other and it had Muslims of all background. Therefore, when in 1906, this deputation called on the Viceroy, it was the most representative Muslim delegation. This delegation was led by **Sir Agha Khan** and **Nawab Mohsin ul Malik** served as a secretary and this delegation met the Viceroy in Simla that was why it was called as Simla Deputation.

The memorandum which they presented was a kind of demands which were the uppermost in the minds of the Muslims at that time. The delegation emphasized that the Muslims should not be viewed simply **in numerical terms** *but they should take into account their* **historical importance** *and the kind of contribution the Muslims had made to British India.*

The delegation also emphasized that **democratic principle** *should be introduced keeping in view the peculiar conditions and circumstances of India. There are different kinds of people living in India and that's the fact that the Muslims have a* **separate entity,** *all these things had to be taken into account and when you introduce some kind of system then these realities had to be accommodated.*

Demands of Simla Deputation

Muslim leaders presented following demands:

1. Representation more than their population because of their importance.
2. Separate electorate
3.   Reservations of Muslims seats in government jobs.
4. Special share in Municipal or district boards University senates and syndicates
5. Muslim representation in Viceroy Executive Council.
6. Muslim University at Aligarh

The Viceroy was sympathetic towards the demands. It encouraged the Muslims to launch struggle for their rights parallel to the Indian National Congress but it required an organized platform. **(This led to the formation of All India Muslim League.)**

Reasons for the formation of MUSLIM LEAGUE:

1. Indifferent Attitude of the Congress towards Muslims: All India National Congress was a pre- dominantly Hindu body. Its interests were always at odds ends to those of the Muslims. By 1906, Muslim leaders were convinced that they must have their own party which may speak for the community on all important occasions.

2. Educational and Economic Backwardness: Muslims had lagged far behind from the Hindus in education and economic progress. Educational and economic conditions could only be up graded by establishing a separate Muslims organization that could represent the wishes of the Muslims.

3. Urdu-Hindi Controversy: The Urdu-Hindu controversy began with the demand of Hindus to replace Urdu by Hindi as official language in Deva Nagari Script. Sir Anthony Macdonal, the then Governor of UP ousted Urdu from public offices. Congress clearly sided with Hindi and supported the movement against Urdu and there was no other political party to support Urdu. Thus, the need of formation of a Muslim political party was felt severely.

4. The Success of Simla Deputation: Minto offered fullest sympathy to the Muslim demands. The success of Deputation compelled the Muslims to have a separate political association of their own.

5. To Save Muslim Entity: The belief uttered by sir Syed Ahmed Khan that the Muslims were somehow a separate entity. The Muslims did not believe that Hindus and Muslims formed one nation. They were different by religion, history, languages and civilization. It became essential for Muslims to establish a political party of their own.

A resolution to form the All India Muslim League was passed by **Nawab Salimullah Khan** and was seconded by Hakim Ajmal Khan, Maulana Muhammad Ali and Moulana Zafar Ali. The resolution was passed by *All India Educational Conference on 30th December 1906*. A committee was formed to prepare its draft constitution. In this way Muslim league was established and become the sole representative of Muslims.

INDIAN NATIONAL CONGRESS:

Founded in 1885 with the objective of obtaining a greater share in government for educated Indians, the Indian National Congress was initially not opposed to British rule. The Congress met once a year during December. It was **Allan Octavian Hume**, who brought about its first meeting in Mumbai, with the approval of Lord Dufferin, the then-Viceroy.

W. C. **Bonerjee** was the first President of the INC. The first Session of INC was held from 28-31 December 1885, and was attended by 72 delegates. A few years down the line, the demands of INC became more radical in the face of constant opposition from the government, and the party became very   active in   the   independence   movement.

In its time as the nation's leader in the freedom struggle, it produced the nation's greatest leaders. Before the Gandhi Era came leaders like Bal Gangadhar Tilak, Bipin Chandra Pal, Lala Lajpat Rai, Gopal Krishna Gokhale, Mohammed Ali Jinnah (later leader of the Muslim League and instrumental in the creation of Pakistan), all starting with the first legendary icon of Indians:

Expected Questions & Answers:

Question No. 1: Explain the reasons for the establishment of the Muslim League in 1906.

7 Nov. 2001, Q.3 b

Question No. 2: Why was the Muslim League founded in 1906?　　　　7 June 2003, Q.2 b

Question No. 3: why was the Muslims League founded in 1906?　　　　7 June 2005, Q.2 b

Question No. 4: why was the Simla delegation of 1906 an important turning for the Muslims of the sub-continent?　　　　7 Nov. 2006 Q.2 b

Question No. 5: Why was the Muslim League established in 1906?　　　　7 June 2009, Q.3 b

Question No. 6: The Muslim League was established in 1906 because the Hindus had their own political party. Do you agree? Give reasons for your answer.　　　　14 June 2010, Q.2 c

Question No. 7: why was the Simla delegation of 1906 an important event for the Muslims of the sub-continent?　　　　7 Nov. 2010 Q.3 b

Question No. 8: why was M.L established in 1906?　　　　7 June 2012 Q.2 b

Question No. 9: Was the need for their own political party the most important reason why the Muslim League was established in 1906? Explain your answer.　　　　14 Nov. 2013 Q.2 c **Question No. 10**: Explain why the Muslim League was formed in 1906.　　　　7 Nov.2014 Q.2 b

Answer to Question No. 2

Muslim league was formed in 1906 to protect & safeguard the rights & interest of Muslims. In the opinion of Dr. K.K Aziz, four factors were responsible for the creation of All India Muslim League.First the old belief uttered by Sir Syed that the Muslims were a separate entity & there should be a protection of Urdu language by any mean, secondly the Hindu character of the Indian national congress which did not allow the Muslims to associate themselves with other Indians. Thirdly, the agitation against the partition of Bengal which conveyed to the Muslims the Hindu designs of domination over the whole of India. Muslims wanted to use the new party as a forum to confront the movement of the Hindus against the partition of Bengal. And finally the Muslim desire to have their exclusive electorate for all representative institution. Muslim intelligentsia believed that it was impossible to acquire the right of separate electorate & due share in government services without political plate form.

So, keeping in view all these reservations the Muhammadan Educational Conference was holding its annual meeting at Dhaka on 30 December 1906, a resolution proposed by Nawab Salim Ullah Khan of Dhaka was unanimously adopted & All India Muslim League was founded.

Topic 11

Minto Morley reforms (Indian Council Act 1909)

Introduction

Lord Minto (Viceroy) & john Morley (secretary Of state) convinced to the demand of increased share in government for Indians. They drew series of reforms in 1909 passed by British parliament as Indian Council act or Morley Minto reforms. It *increased membership of legislative councils* in both the central and provincial governments. Importantly, educated men who paid a certain sum of taxes were allowed to *vote* for the first time in Indian history. Some seats were *reserved for Muslim candidates*, and only Muslims could vote for them. Moreover, the elected members were also empowered to question officials; to debate legislation, including the budget; and to introduce laws. However, the viceroy and the governors still had total control and could veto any laws that were passed. This act and other measures gradually restored calm to India. The act is important because it established representative responsible government for India.

main features of the Act of 1909

The following were the main features of the Act of 1909:

1. The number of the members of the Legislative Council at the Center was increased from 16 to 60.

2. The number of the members of the Provincial Legislatives was also increased. It was fixed as 50 in the provinces of Bengal, Madras and Bombay, and for the rest of the provinces it was 30.

3. Right of separate electorate was given to the Muslims.

4. The members of the Legislative Councils were permitted to discuss the budgets, suggest the amendments and even to vote on them.

5. Two Indians were nominated to the Council of the Secretary of State for Indian Affairs.

6. The Governor General was empowered to nominate one Indian member to his Executive Council.

Expected Questions & Answers

Question No. 1: The Morley Minto reforms were the most important of the attempts by the Muslims, Hindus or the British Governments in seeking a solution to the problems in the Sub Continent between 1906 & 1920? Do you agree? Give reason for your answer. 14
June 2003 Q. 2 c

Question No. 2: Why did the congress party oppose the Morley Minto reforms of 1909? 7
November 2001 Q. 2 b

Question No. 3: Were the Morley Minto reforms the most important attempt by the Muslim, the Hindus or the British in seeking a solution to the problems in the sub continent between 1906 & 1920? Explain your answer. 14 November 2005 Q.3 c

Question No. 4: the Morley Minto reforms were more important than any other political developments between 1909 & 1919. Do you agree or disagree? Give reasons to your answer. 14 November 2007 Q. 3 c

Question No. 5: why did Congress oppose the Morley Minto reforms of 1909? 7 November 2008 Q.2 c

Question No. 6: The Lucknow Pact of 1916 was the most important attempt by either the Muslims, Hindus or the British government in seeking a solution to the problems in the sub-continent between 1909 and 1919.' Do you agree? Give reasons for your answer. Oct/Nov 2012 Q.2 c 14

Question No. 7: How successful were political developments in finding a solution to the problems in the sub-continent between 1909 and 1919? Explain your answer. 14 May/June 2014 Q. 2 c

Answer to question No 1:

Morley Minto Reforms 1909 were a definite improvement & advance on the act of 1892. It was an important step in the direction or representation & responsible government. But Minto Morley reforms didn't solve the problems in the sub continent. Therefore it is not possible to agree with the statement, because the demand of the *self-rule* was not granted. But From the British government point of view it can be said that these reforms increased the members of the central legislative assembly from 16 to 60 & first time an Indian was included in Viceroy's Executive Council. But the reforms didn't introduce *democracy* in the country. It only allowed some opportunity to a limited number of Indians to participate in law making & administration with limited powers.

The legislative had no control over Executive. The assemblies could pass resolutions in the form recommendations which *viceroy* or Governors (in province) could accept or could not accept. The number of *voters* was very small & system of voting was discriminatory. The congress was not satisfied because the aim of self rule was still very far. One Indian member was added to viceroy's Executive Council & one to each of provincial Councils. The Congress condemned the reforms but agreed to work with them. Muslims were satisfied over the grant of separate electorate in the 1909 reforms because it protected Muslim rights to some extent.

In 1913 Muslim league added self rule to its demands. it brought the congress & ML closer. Mr. Jinnah joined the ML in 1913 & since then he made very strong efforts to bring the two parties closer so that achieving of self-rule may be easier. The annual meetings of Congress & ML were held at Lucknow in 1916 & leaders of both parties came to some agreements. The Congress accepted the right of separate electorate for Muslims & the one third seats in the central assembly were to be given to Muslims. Both parties demanded that elected members in both Central & Provincial assemblies would be in majority. They also agreed upon autonomy for provinces & on the principle of weightage.

In 1909 the Minto Morley reforms had promised that more powers will be given to Indians after 10 years. Therefore in 1919 Reforms more concessions were given. A system of two houses was proposed for the Central Legislature. Number of members was greatly increased & elected members were to be in majority. The 1919 reforms introduced the system of Diarchy in provinces. According to this system the unimportant or transferred subjects (agriculture, education, and health) were given to Indian ministers. Important or reserved subjects (police, Justice, Revenue) were under the control of the Governors & Executive Councilors who were British. Three Indian members were introduced in Viceroy's Executive Council. Although the number of voters was increased, yet the right to vote was still discriminatory. These reforms also disappointed both the ML & the Congress because both had hoped for more substantial powers. The Viceroy and Governors had vast powers to appoint ministers & to dismiss the assemblies. In short the Act of 1919 didn't do much to solve the constitutional problem of India.

We come to the conclusion that the Lucknow Pact 1916 was the most important political development between 1909 & 1919. under the Lucknow Pact both the congress & ML were moving in the right direction with cooperation & understanding. If both the parties maintained their cooperation & concession to each other the goal of self rule or independence would have been achieved much earlier.

ANSWER TO QUESTION NO. 2:

The congress opposed and rejected the MMR of 1909 because congress has stared demanding **self- rule** and independence of India while the reforms didn't give any inclination to give any effective power to Indian to run the government.

Besides that, the reforms granted separate electorate to the Muslims. The congress was in favour of joint electorates. The congress claimed that it represented all Indian people and that separate electorate was undemocratic. Some Hindus also resented the relative high position of Muslims in the councils despite their much smaller numbers.

Besides that the Viceroy's council had no real power. They could only discuss and debate an issue and present their opinion in the form of suggestions. The real power rested with the viceroy and governor of provinces. Therefore congress opposed MMR of 1909.

The Lucknow Pact 1916 Joint demands to the British

What was the Lucknow pact?

Lucknow Pact refers to an agreement between the Indian National Congress and the Muslim League. In 1916, **Muhammed Ali Jinnah**, a member of the Muslim League, negotiated with the Indian National Congress to reach an agreement to pressure the British government to adopt a more liberal approach to India and give Indians more authority to run their country. This was a considerable change of policy for the Muslim League (not to loyal British), as its position had been that to preserve Muslim interests in India. After the unpopular partition of Bengal, the Muslim League was confused about its stand and it was at this time that Jinnah approached the League. Jinnah was the mastermind and architect of the pact and signed it with Congress led by **Mahajan**. The agreement was confirmed by the annual sessions of the Congress and the League in their annual sessions held at Lucknow on December 29 and December 31, 1916 respectively. **Sarojini Naidu** gave Jinnah, the chief architect of the Lucknow Pact, the title of "the *Ambassador of Hindu-Muslim Unity*".

Why was the Lucknow pact made?

Muslims' New Strategy after reversal of partition of Bengal
When Bengal was partitioned in 1905, Hindus reacted against the decision and they went on violent protests and boycotts of British goods. On the other hand, the Muslims remained loyal to the British rule. The British could not sustain the pressure of demonstrations and reversed the decision of partition in 1911. This was a betrayal to the Muslims' loyalty. They realized the British rulers could no longer be trusted. Now they had to devise a new strategy for achieving their goals. They wanted to turn towards the demand of **self-rule** but they needed constitutional protection – separate electorate and provincial autonomy – from Hindus after the British would leave India. Muslim League, therefore, signed the Lucknow Pact in 1916 in which Congress agreed on granting the Muslims 1/3 reserved seats in the central legislative council.

Jinnah's Role and liberal leadership
At the time of the pact, Muhammad Ali Jinnah was an *idealist* who believed that Hindus and Muslims could work together. He wanted that all religious groups should live together in harmony. He was a strong supporter of Hindu-Muslim unity. He believed that *joint demands* would put more pressure on the British. Therefore he persuaded the Congress and the Muslim League for the Lucknow Pact in 1916. He believed that this pact would lead to   united   Indian nation.
(Note: Mr. Jinnah became realist after Nehru Report in 1929 who then believed in the two- nation theory).

Joint Demand
Congress was keen to gain the support of Muslim League for its demand of
self-rule in India. It hoped that it would be difficult for the British to reject the joint demand

of self-rule for longer time. Therefore, it was ready to give concessions to Muslim League for its own objective of home-rule. That is why Congress went into Lucknow Pact with Muslim League in 1916.

Main clauses of the Lucknow Pact

1. There shall be *self-government* in India.

1.   Muslims should be given *one-third* representation in the central government.

2. There should be *separate electorates* for all the communities until a community demanded joint electorates.

3. A system of *weightage* should be adopted.

4. The number of the members of Central Legislative Council should be increased to 150.

5. The size of provincial legislatures should not be extended.

6. *Voting* rights for all

7. No bill concerning a community should be passed if the bill is opposed by three-fourth of the members of that community in the Legislative Council.

8. The term of the Legislative Council should be five years.

9.   Half of the members of Imperial Legislative Council should be Indians.

10. The Executive should be separated from the Judiciary.

Although this Hindu Muslim Unity did not last more than eight years, and collapsed after the development of differences between the two communities after the Khilafat Movement, yet it was an important event in the history of the Muslims of South Asia. It was the first time that the Congress recognized the Muslim League as the political party representing the Muslims of the region.

Importance of the Pact:

- Movements towards self rule.
- Hindus & Muslims together made demand to British for the first time.
- Hindus accepted partition for self governing India.
- Muslims could protect their rights if they worked with congress.
- Self government was possible.
- In 1917, two Home Rule leagues campaigned in India, one by Tilak & other by Ainnie Basant.
- The pact marked the high water mark of Hindu Muslim unity.

Jinnah said that the pact had come about because, *'cooperation in the cause of our motherland should be our guiding principle. India's real progress can only be achieved by a true understanding & harmonious relations between the two great sister communities'*.

Expected Questions & answers:

Question No. 1: Explain why the Lucknow pact of 1916 was made?   7
November 2000 Q. 3 b

Question No. 2: which of the following had the most important effect on Hindu Muslim relationship between 1914 & 1928.
    (i)   Lucknow Pact (ii) Montague Chelmsford Reforms 1919 (iii) Nehru Report?
    Explain your answer with reference to all three of the above.14 June 2001 Q.3 c

Question No. 3: The Lucknow pact of 1916 was the only beacon of hope of Hindu Muslim unity between 1914 & 1930.Do you agree? Give reasons for your answer.14November 2004 Q. 2 c

Question No. 4: Explain why the Lucknow Pact of 1916 came about.7 June 2006 Q.2 b

Question No. 5: During the First World War, Congress and the Muslim League had moved closer together, partly due to the failure of the British to grant more rights to the Indians before 1914. During the war, the British realised that concessions had to be made and let it be known that they were proposing a number of these. The Muslim League and Congress then met together at Lucknow.
(a) What was the Lucknow Pact?4 June 2012 Q. 2 a

Question No. 6:'The Lucknow Pact of 1916 was the most important attempt by the Muslims, Hindus or the British government in seeking a solution to the problems in the sub-continent between 1909 and 1919.' Do you agree? Give reasons for your answer.   14
November 2012 Q.2 c

Question No. 7: Explain why the Lucknow Pact of 1916 came about.   7
June 2013 Q.3 b

Answer to question No.3:

Lucknow pact was the only hope for the Hindu-Muslim unity between 1914 & 1930.A firm foundation was laid for the political advance of Muslims & the way was also opened for joint efforts by Hindus &Muslims for the attainment of the goal of self government. That was the first & last pact concluded between the two parties on the question of separate electorates & modalities of form of government in India. It created conclusive environment for the launching of joint anti imperialist movement & carried great constitutional significance in future.

The Hindus agreed to the right of separate electorate for the Muslims for the first & the last time. The Hindus conceded that the Muslims would have 1/3 representation in the imperial Legislative council. A weightage formula was proposed under which the Muslim would get less representation than their population in the legislative council in those provinces where they were in majority but more in those provinces where they were in minority. Similarly Hindus would be given more seats in Punjab & Bengal where Hindus were in minority. Provincial autonomy was also agreed upon.

Thus both parties gave concession to each other & a spirit of cooperation prevailed. All these measures were such that had the Congress adhered to the pact & had given proper adequate share to Muslims in political power; the history of the sub continent would have been different. Perhaps independence could have been achieved much earlier & even the partition of the country could have been avoided.

But unfortunately the congress leaders didn't stick to the Lucknow pact & started showing their resentment to separate electorate after a few years. Thus we find that in Nehru report (1928) the system of joint electorate was suggested replacing separate electorate. Unitary form of government was suggested for the country with powers with majority power. Reservation of seats for Muslims in Central assembly & the concept of weightage were abolished. All these steps made the gulf between Muslims & Hindus much wider & unbridgeable.
Mr. Jinnah suggested three reasonable amendments in the Nehru report in order to safeguard Muslims interests but these were rejected by the congress. Muslims become cautious & lost all trust with congress leadership. The Nehru report shattered all hopes of Hindu Muslim unity & Mr. Jinnah remarked that *"it was parting of ways"*.
Thus it correct to say that Lucknow pact was the only opportunity & hope for Hindu Muslim unity.

The Montague Chelmsford Reforms (Indian Council Act 1919)

Introduction

In World War I, the British claimed that they stood for the protection of **democracy** around the world. Thus the Indians, who fought for them in this war, demanded that democracy should also be introduced in their country. **Lord Montague, the Secretary of State** for Indian Affairs said that in order to satisfy the local demands, his government was interested in giving more representation to the natives in India. New reforms would be introduced in the country to meet this objective. Finally, in cooperation with the **Governor General Lord Chelmsford**, Montague presented a report on the constitutional reforms for India in 1918. The report was discussed and approved by the British Parliament and then became the Act of 1919. This Act is commonly known as Montague- Chelmsford Reforms.

Main features of the Act of 1919

The following were the main features of the Act of 1919:

- The **Central Legislature** was to consist of *two houses*, **Upper House** (Council of the State), and the **Lower House** (Legislative Assembly). Council of the State was to consist of 60 members. The Legislative Assembly was to consist of 144 members. The duration of the Upper House was five and of the Lower House was three years.
- **Powers** were divided between the center and the provinces.
- The system of **'Diarchy'** or a kind of double government in the Provinces was introduced.
- The Governor General had the power to nominate as many members to his Executive Council as he wanted.
- The franchise was limited.
- Both the houses had equal legislative powers. In case of a tie, the Governor General was to call a joint meeting where the matter was to be decided by majority vote.
- The Executive Council was not responsible to Legislate.
- Provincial Legislatures were supposed to be unicameral.
- Besides Muslims, other minorities including Sikhs, Anglo-Indians, Christians and Europeans were also given the right of separate electorate.
- New reforms were to be introduced after ten years.
- The **Council** of the Secretary of State was to comprise of eight to twelve people. Three of them should be Indian.

INDIANS RESPONSE:

Indian Constitutional Act of 1919 was passed to satisfy Indian people. On the contrary, Indian people opposed it because the Act went against Congress-League pact thus resulting in the Hindu opposition. Muslims partly accepted the Montague-Chelmsford reforms with certain reservations and demands regarding the safety of Muslim states. Gandhi categorically rejected this scheme and congress denounced it *as inadequate, unsatisfactory and disappointing*. Besides these problems, the events like Rowlatt act, the Jallianwal Bagh tragedy and Khilafat movement further aggravated the situation and doomed the reforms to failure.

DIARCHY:

Diarchy was introduced as a constitutional reform by Edwin Samuel Montagu (secretary of state for India, 1917–22) and Lord Chelmsford (viceroy of India, 1916–21).

According to Diarchy the various fields or subjects of administration were divided between the British councillors and the Indian ministers, being named **reserved** and **transferred** subjects, respectively. The reserved subjects came under the heading of law and order and included justice, police, land revenue, and irrigation. The transferred subjects (i.e., those under the control of Indian ministers) included local self-government, education, public health, public works, and agriculture, forests, and fisheries. The system ended with the introduction of provincial autonomy in 1935.

AMRITSAR MASSACRE 1919:

Massacre of Amritsar, (April 13, 1919), incident in which British troops fired on a crowd of unarmed Indian protesters, killing a large number. It left a permanent scar on Indo-British relations.

In 1919 the British government of India enacted the Rowlett Acts, extending its World War I emergency powers to combat revolutionary activities. At Amritsar in Punjab, about 10,000 demonstrators unlawfully protesting these measures confronted troops commanded by Gen. **Dyer** in an open space known as the **Jallianwalla Bagh**, which had only one exit. (The site is now a national monument.) The troops fired on the crowd, killing an estimated 379 and wounding about 1,200 according to one official report The **Hunter Commission** condemned General Dyer in 1920, but the House of Lords praised his action, and a fund was raised in his honour.

Q.No.1: Towards the end of the First World War the British decided that firm action was needed to keep a grip on India, especially with the threat of renewed violence. During the war the British had the Defence of India Act to help keep order. Once this Act had expired the Rowlatt Act was introduced.

Describe the Rowlatt Act.   4
M/J 2011 Q.3 a

Q.No.2: The Montague-Chelmsford reforms were more important than any other political developments between 1909 and 1919.' Do you agree or disagree? Give reasons for your answer.   14
O/N 2011 Q.3 c

Topic 14
KHILAFAT MOVEMENT 1919-1924

Introduction

The Khilafat movement was a very important event in the political history of India. The Muslims of India had a great regard for the Khilafat (Caliphate) which was held by the Ottoman Empire. During World War I, the Ottoman Empire (Turkey) joined the **war** in favour of Germany. But Turkey and Germany lost the war and a pact commonly known as *Istanbul Accord* was concluded between the Allied Forces on 3rd November 1918. According to this Pact the territories of Turkey were to be divided among France, Greece and Britain. That resented Muslim a lot and khilafat movement began.

During the war the Indian Muslims were in a very awkward position, because they had a deep-rooted devotion to the caliphate. They had profound respect for this **holy** institution. Therefore, their support to the British Government was subject to the safeguard and protection of the holy places of Turkey and on the condition that Turkey will not to be deprived of its territories. But the British Government could not fulfil both of these promises. The **Treaty of Savers 1920** was imposed on Turkey and its territories were distributed among European countries. A wave of anger swept across the Muslin World and the Indian Muslims rose against the British Government. Muslim leaders like *Maulana Abdul Kalam Azad, Moulana Muhammad Ali Johar, Moulana Shoukat Ali* and others reacted against the British Government policy and were put behind the bars.

Aims of Khilafat Movement

Thus, Muslims organized a mass movement, which came to be known as Khilafat Movement. The aims of this movement were

(a) To protect the Holy place of Turkey

(b) To restore the Territories of Turkey

(c) To restore the Ottoman Empire.

Besides that **congress support** also remained very encouraging for Muslims to launch khilafat movement. In December 1919 both the Khilafat Committee and Congress held their meetings simultaneously at Amritsar and a delegation was prepared which was sent to England under the leadership of Maulana Mohammad Ali Johar to see the British Prime Minister and to explain the Indian point of view regarding the Khilafat. The delegation visited England in 1920. The leaders of the delegation addressed the House of Commons and saw the British Prime Minister, Lloyd George who paid no heed to the delegations demand. The delegation stayed at London for eight months and won many hearts and sympathies of people in Britain delivering speeches. However, the delegation returned to India unsuccessful in October 1920.

After the unsuccessful visit to England the leaders of Khilafat Movement realized the fact that British were not in the mood to help them. Therefore, they realized that a new strategy needed to be adopted. With this aim they decided to launch a movement of Non Co-operation. When the leaders of Khilafat movement announced the Non Co-operation Movement, the Congress extended its full support to the Khilafat Movement. The leaders of the two met at Amritsar and resolved to launch a country wide agitation under the leadership of Mr. Gandhi.

Khilafat conferences:

First Khilafat Conference: November 1919 in Delhi.

- Main leaders were Maulana Mohammad Ali Johar, Moulana Shaukat Ali & Moulana Abul Kalam Azad, and Ghandi.
- Main aim was to persuade British to keep their promises about maintaining the Turkish Empire.
- Resolution was passed and everyone agreed in sending a delegation to Britain to make sure that the British were aware of Muslim strength of Muslims support for the Khalifa.
- Muslims also boycotted British goods besides Hindus and adopted a policy of non-cooperation with them.
- Gandhi was an advocate of policy of passive resistance. He gave this approach the name 'Satyagraya', meaning *"not meek submission to the will of evil door but the pitting of one's whole soul against the will of the tyrant".*
- Gandhi urged Muslims to joining Congress in seeking 'Swaraj' (self-rule) for India.

Second Khilafat Conference:
December 1919, Amritsar.
It was decided that all three organizations (Muslim League, Congress & Khilafat people) would be working together to oppose plans to dismember the Turkish Empire.

- Maulana Muhammad Ali visited Britain & insisted the Britain not to punish Turkey but the Prime Minister Lloyd George said *"Austria has had justice; Germany has had justice-pretty terrible justice –why should Turkey escape"?*

Mehmed VI :

Mehmed VI (14 January 1861 – 16 May 1926) was the 36th and last Sultan of the Ottoman Empire, reigning from 1918 to 1922. His father was Sultan Abdulmecid I .Mehmed was removed from the throne when the Ottoman sultanate was abolished in 1922.
The First World War was a disaster for the Ottoman Empire. British and allied forces had conquered **Baghdad, Damascus, and Jerusalem** during the war and most of the Empire was divided among the European allies. In April 1920 British were granted over Palestine .On 10 August 1920, Mehmed's representatives signed the Treaty of Sevres, which recognized the mandates and recognized Hejaz as an independent state.
Turkish nationalists rejected the settlement by Sultan. A new government, the Turkish Grand National Assembly, under the leadership of Mustafa Kemal (Ataturk) was formed on 23 April 1920, in Ankara . The new government denounced the rule of Mehmed VI and a temporary constitution was drafted. The Turkish Grand National Assembly also abolished the Sultanate on 1 November 1922, and Mehmed was expelled from Constantinople. He went into exile in Malta. Mehmed died on 16 May 1926 in Italy, and was buried at Damascus.

MUSTAFA KAMAL ATATURK:

Mustafa Kemal Ataturk 19 May 1881 – 10 November 1938) was a Turkish army officer, reformist statesman, and the first President of Turkey. He is credited with being the founder of the Republic of Turkey. His surname, Ataturk (meaning "Father of the Turks"), was granted to him in 1934 and forbidden to any other person by the Turkish parliament.

Ataturk was a military officer during I WW. Ataturk then embarked upon a program of political, economic, and cultural reforms, seeking to transform the former Ottoman Empire into a modern and secular nation-state. Under his leadership, thousands of new schools were built, primary education was made free and compulsory, and women were given equal civil and political rights, while the burden of taxation on peasants was reduced.

His government also carried out an extensive policy of Turkification. The principles of Ataturk's reforms, upon which modern Turkey was established, are referred to as Kemalism.

Expected Questions and Answers

Question No. 1: Was the migration of Afghanistan the most important reason behind the failure of A Khilafat Movement? 14June 2000. Q. 3 c

Question No. 2: Explain the reasons for the establishment of the Khilafat Movement. 7November 2001. Q.2 b

Question No. 3: Why was the Khilafat Movement founded?7June 2002, Q.3 b

Question No. 4: Was the withdrawal of Gandhi's support from the Khilafat Movement the most important reason

for its

Question No. 6: Was the Chaura Chauri incident of 1922 the most important reason for the failure of the Khilafat movement? Give reasons for your answer.   14   June 2004 Q.2c

Question No. 7: Was the Khilafat Movement founded because the Muslims feared the break up of Turkey after the 1st

world war? Explain your answer.   14   June 2005 Q. 2 c

Question No. 8: Explain why the Khilafat movement has failed by 1924.   7   June 2006 Q.3 b

Question No. 9: Was the abolition of the institution of the caliphate in 1924 the main reason for the failure of the Khilafat Movement? Give reasons for answer.   14   November 2006 Q. 2 c

Question No. 10: The Khilafat movement failed by 1924 because of poor leadership .Do you agree? Give reasons for your

answer.   14   November 2008 Q. 2 c

Question No.11: Explain the reasons for the failure of the K.M.   7   June 2009 Q.4 b

Question No.12: Why was the Khilafat Movement founded?   7   June 2010 Q.2 b

Question No.13: Was the migration of Afghanistan the most important reason why the Khilafat Movement failed? Explain your answer.   14   Nov. 2010. Q. 3 c

Question No.14: A number of events that happened during the years of the Khilafat Movement led to its failure. During the years when the Movement was at its strongest, western dress and hair styles became less popular and the idea grew that disregard of the law of Islam by the British made India a dar-ul-harb(enemy territory). Thus thousands of Muslims set off on their hijrat.

Describe the hijrat.   4   Nov. 2011 Q.3 a

Question No.15: 'The Khilafat Movement failed by 1924 because Gandhi withdrew his support.' Do you agree? Give

reasons for your answer.   14   June 2012 Q.2 c

Question No.16: The Khilafat Movement started because of the treatment of Turkey by the British after the First

World War. Turkey was a Muslim country, and its ruler, the Sultan, was considered to be the Khalifa, the head of the worldwide Islamic community. When the British threatened to take territory away from the Khalifa, the Muslims of India were outraged and formed the Khilafat Movement to protect the Sultan and their religion. One of the events that took place during this Movement was the Chauri-Chaura incident.

Describe the Chauri-Chaura incident.	4	Nov. 2012 Q. 3 a
Question No.17: Why did the Khilafat Movement fail by 1924?	7	Nov. 2013 Q.3 b

Answer to question No. 9

The abolition of the institution of Caliphate by the Turks themselves remained the most important reason for the failure of Khilafat Movement. **Mustafa Kamal Ataturk** ,the Turkish leader established a modern democratic government in Turkey with a properly elected parliament. In this set up the caliph & the seat of Caliphate had no place. The caliph was deposed & exiled in 1924. Muslims in India were perplexed & found their movement cut at its base. Muslims in India had nothing to fight for & the khilafat Movement ended in failure in 1924.

Besides that the movement got many other set backs on account of many reasons. In 1920 the congress also started *non-cooperation movement*. The congress joined hands with the khiilafat movement because both were against the British. Khilafat movement got much strength from the support of the congress. Joint protest meetings & processions of Muslims & Hindus together became a common feature throughout the sub- continent. In1922 a procession at **Chauri Chura**(a small town in eastern U.P) was in progress. The mob became violent & set a police station on fire in which 22 policemen were burnt alive. Mr. Ghandhi suddenly called off the non-cooperation movement without consulting anyone & without taking the Muslims into confidence. The Muslims were greatly discouraged at the loss of Congress support. Khilafat Movement was weakened. Mr Jinaah had opposed the non-cooperation movement saying that it would lead to violence, and the same happened. Mr. Jinnah resigned from the Congress in 1920.

The movement got other threats as well. The **Hijrat Movement** (1921), an off shoot of Khilafat Movement failed badly. Some ulemas had declared that India was Dar-al-Harb & it was better for Muslims to live in an independent Muslim country. Therefore some 18000 Muslims mostly from NWFP sold their belongings & sought asylum in Afghanistan .In the beginning the migrants were welcomed but soon later Afghan government refused to admit them. Many perished & others returned penniless & homeless.

Another tragic event was the *Moplah Uprising* which remained *responsible for the failure of Khilafat Movement. It also affected Hindu Muslim relationship.* In mid of August 1921, agrarian riots broke out in Nilambur. The Moplah peasants revolted against the Hindu landlord's oppressive policies, which are in alliance with the British. The Hindu landlords redistributed their lands and the Moplahs, who had been suffering, rose in revolt. A pitched battle between the British regiment and the Moplahs killed several Europeans. Four thousand Moplahs were killed in action and tens of thousands were injured. Then there was the notorious *Moplah Train Tragedy*. Around a hundred prisoners, confined in a closed and almost airtight goods van, were transported by rail. When the door was opened, 66 Moplahs were found suffocated to death and the remaining 34 were on the verge of collapse.

The British government also arrested the *leader*s of the Khilafat Movement on account of their anti-government speeches & the movement was deprived of their effective & strong leadership, both Hindu and Muslim leaders were imprisoned for several years. About 30000 workers all over India were put in jails. The movement slows down. The movement was **unrealistic** & was bound to fail. The caliphate & the people of Turkey had no interest in the politics of India. Therefore agitations & protests in India were to affect the events in turkey. Far sighted people like Mr. Jinnah & Allama Iqbal didn't support the movement.

But the most important reason for the failure of the Khilafat Movement was the abolition of the institution of Caliphate by the Turks themselves. Mustafa Kamal Ataturk ,the Turkish leader established a modern democratic government in Turkey with a properly elected parliament. In this set up the caliph & the seat of Caliphate had no place. The caliph was deposed & exiled in 1924. Muslims in India had nothing to fight for & the khilafat Movement ended in failure in 1924.Therefore the abolition of the institution of caliphate in 1924 was the main reason for the failure of the khilafat Movement.

SIMON COMMISSION, NEHRU REPORT, 14 POINTS OF JINNAH

JINNAH'S DEHLI PROPOSALS MARCH 1927:

1: Sind should be separated from Bombay and should be constituted into an independent province.
2: Reforms should be introduced in the North-West Frontier Province and Baluchistan on the same footing as in any other province of India.
3: Reservation of seats according to the population for different communities in the Punjab and Bengal.
4: Muslims should be given 1/3rd representation in the Central Legislature.

THE SIMON COMMISSION 1927

- The government of India act 1919 stated that a commission was going to be set up after 10 years to enquire the working of the Montague Chelmsford Reforms.
- Conservative Government feared to lose power to the Labor part so it decided to bring date of Simon Commission forward.
- In 1927 a seven men committee was formed under the supervision of John Simon to consider India's situation. All of them were British. Composition of committee was considered insult in India. And for that reason immediate protest was raised from all the important political parties. When the Simon Commission arrived, the local masses welcomed it by with slogans of "Go back Simon!". All the major political parties of Sub-continent, except the Shafi League of Punjab, boycotted the Simon Commission.

- All parties decided to settle their differences & work in opposition to the Simon commission.
- In May 1928, Congress, ML, Liberals, Hindu Mahasaba & Sikh league met in all part conference to draft constitution which Indian people thought to govern their country and finally Nehru report was introduced.
- Motilal Nehru headed this committee. There were nine other members in this committee including two Muslims, **Syed Ali Imam and Shoaib Qureshi.**

There were following recommendations on Commissions report:

1. The Diarchy system in the provinces should be abolished.
2. The power of the central government and the provincial governors should be reduced.
3. Federal system of government should be introduced in India.
4. The right to vote should be extended to more people.
5. The separation of Sindh was not granted.
6. The demand of the frontier for equal status was also neglected.

NEHRU REPORT 1928

The following were the recommendations advanced by the Nehru Report:

1. India should be given the status of a **dominion.**

2. There should be **federal form of government** in India.

3. India should have a parliamentary form of government.

4. There should be bi-cameral legislature.

5. There should be **no separate electorate** for any community.

6. System of weightage for minorities should be rejected.

7. Reservation of Muslim seats should not be maintained.

8. Muslims should enjoy **one-fourth** representation in the Central Legislature.

9. Sindh should be separated from Bombay.

10. The N. W. F. P. should be given full provincial status.

11. **Hindi** should be made the official language of India.

The recommendations of the Nehru Report went against the interests of the Muslim community. It was an attempt to serve Hindu predominance over Muslims. The Nehru Committee's greatest blow was the rejection of separate electorates. If the report had taken into account the Delhi Proposals, the Muslims might have accepted it. But the Nehru Committee did not consider the Delhi Proposals at all while formulating their report. The Muslims were asking for one-third representation in the center while Nehru Committee gave them only one-fourth representation. It is true that two demands of Muslims were considered in the Nehru Report but both of them incomplete. It was said that Sindh should be separated from Bombay but the condition of self-economy was also put forward. It demanded constitutional reforms in N. W. F. P. but Baluchistan was overlooked in the report.

Of the two Muslim members of the Nehru Committee, **Syed Ali Imam** could attend only one meeting due to his illness and **Shoaib Qureshi** did not endorse views of the Committee on the issue of Muslim representation in legislature. Thus the Nehru Report was nothing else than a Congress document and thus totally opposed by Muslims of the Sub-continent. The Hindus under Congress threatened the government with a disobedience movement if the Nehru report was not implemented into the Act by December 31, 1929. This Hindu attitude proved to be a milestone in the freedom movement of the Muslims. It also proved to be a turning point in the life of Muhammad Ali Jinnah. After reading the Nehru Report, Jinnah announced a **'parting of the ways' and introduced his famous 14 points.** The Nehru Report reflected the inner prejudice and narrow-minded approach of the Hindus.

JINNAH'S 14 POINTS 1929:

Quaid-i-Azam presented his famous Fourteen Points in 1929 to counter Nehru report. These points were as follows:

1. The form of the future constitution should be federal with the powers vested in the provinces.

2. Autonomy shall be granted to all provinces.

3. Adequate and effective representation of minorities in every province.

4. In the Central Legislative, Muslim representation shall not be less than one-third.

5. Right of separate electorate for Muslims.

6. Any territorial distribution that might at any time be necessary shall not in any way affect the Muslim majority in the Punjab, Bengal and the North West Frontier Province.

7. Full religious liberty.

8. No bill or any resolution shall be passed in any legislature if three-fourth of the members of that community oppose such a bill.

9. Sindh should be separated from the Bombay presidency.

10. Reforms should be introduced in the North West Frontier Province and Baluchistan on the same footing as in the other provinces.

11. Muslims should be given an adequate share, in all the services of the state.

12. Adequate safeguards for the protection of Muslim culture and for the protection and

promotion of Muslim education, language, religion, personal laws.

13. No cabinet, either central or provincial, should be formed without there being a proportion of at least one-third Muslim ministers.

14. No change shall be made in the constitution by the Central Legislature without the approval of Indian Federation.

KEY POINTS:

- Mr. Jinnah presented his 14 points at the annual meeting of Muslim League in 1929.
- These 14 points were given to safeguard & protect the interest of Muslims.
- The demand of separate electorate, establishment of province of Sindh, giving proper status to NWFP & Baluchistan were to be strengthen the Muslims majority areas & were important steps towards giving proper identity to the Muslim nation.
- The Nehru report had created a great deal of confusion in the Muslims who started thinking seriously for the attainment of a separate homeland for the Muslims.
- The 14 points showed the Muslims their eventual objective & destination.

Expected Question & Answers:

Question No. 1: why did Jinnah produce his 14 points in 1929?

7
June 2005.Q.3 b

Question No. 2: was the introduction of Jinnah's 14 points in 1929 the most important factor in the development of the Pakistan Movement between 1928 & 1935? Give reasons for your answer.   14
June 2006, Q. 3 c

Question No.3: why did Jinnah produce his 14 points in 1929?

7
Nov.2007 Q.3 b

Question No.4: The 14 points were M.Ali Jinnah's greatest achievement in the years 1929 to 1947, do you agree? Explain your answer.

1
4
June 2009, Q. 4 c

Question No.5: Describe the Nehru Report.   4
June 2011, Q.4 a

Question No.6: The declaration of the Day of Deliverance in 1939 was Muhammad Ali Jinnah's greatest achievement in the years 1929 to 1947.' Do you agree? Explain your answer.   14
Nov.2012 Q.3 c

Question No.7: In 1927 the British government set up a commission chaired by Sir John Simon as provided for under the terms of the 1919 Government of India Act. The commission was to look into the situation in India but none of its members was an Indian. This was considered an insult by the Congress party which decided to boycott the commission.

(a) What was the Nehru Report?   [4]

Nov 2014 Q.3 a

Answer to Questions No 1 & 3:

The recommendation of the Nehru report was a source of disappointments for the Muslims. Muslims leaders who had always been anxious to ensure the protection of Muslim interest could not remain silent. Its three main points rather demands were totally against the interest of the Muslims, like the demand of unitary form of government in India, Joint electorates & introduction of Hindi as national language.

Mr. Jinnah suggested three amendments in Nehru report which were rejected. Therefore Jinnah put forward the 14 points in answer to the Nehru report (Jinnah also called the Nehru report as the parting of the ways). These points were produced in order to protect the political rights of Muslims. These points were quite comprehensive & covered all aspects of Muslim demands at that time.

In the 14 points Jinnah demanded Federal form of government, provincial autonomy, separate electorate, effective representation of Muslims in assemblies & 1/3rd seats for Muslims in all cabinets. Creation of new Muslim provinces of Sind, NWFP, & Baluchistan was also demanded.

Jinnah's 14 points clearly reflected the demands, sentiments & aspirations of the Muslims. But as in the past, the congress did not give them any importance & instead determined to oppose them. Anyhow 14 points became the part of government of India act 1935 later on.

THE ROUND TABLE CONFERENCES 1930-1932

Introduction

There had been a series of meetings in three sessions called by the British government to consider the future constitution of India in 1930 to 1932. The conference resulted from a review of the Government of India Act of 1919, undertaken in 1927 by the Simon Commission, whose report was published in 1929. The conferences were held in London.

The Indian political community received the Simon Commission Report with great resentment. Different political parties gave vent to their feelings in different ways.

The Congress started a Civil Disobedience Movement (salt March) under Gandhi's command. The Muslims reserved their opinion on the Simon Report declaring that the report was not final and the matters should decided after consultations with the leaders representing all communities in India.

The Indian political situation seemed deadlocked. The British government refused to contemplate any form of self-government for the people of India. This caused frustration amongst the masses, who often expressed their anger in violent clashes.

The **Labor Government** returned to power in Britain, and a glimmer of hope ran through Indian hearts. Labor leaders had always been sympathetic to the Indian cause. The government decided to hold a Round Table Conference in London to consider new constitutional reforms. All Indian politicians; Hindus, Muslims, Sikhs and Christians were summoned to London for the conference.

First Round Table Conference

The first session of the conference opened in London on November 12, 1930. The Round Table Conference was opened officially by **King George V** and chaired by the British Prime Minister, **Ramsay MacDonald.** The three British political parties were represented by sixteen delegates. All parties from India were present except for the Congress, whose leaders were in jail due to the Civil Disobedience Movement. Congress leaders stated that they would have nothing to do with further constitutional discussion unless the Nehru Report was enforced in its entirety as the constitution of India. Almost **89** members attended the conference, out of which 58 were chosen from various communities and interests in British India, and the rest from princely states and other political parties. The prominent among the Muslim delegates invited by the British government were Sir Aga Khan, Quaid-i-Azam, Maulana Muhammad Ali Jouhar, Sir Muhammad Shafi and Maulvi Fazl-i-Haq. Sir Taj Bahadur Sapru, Mr. Jaikar and Dr. Moonje were outstanding amongst the Hindu leaders.

It was agreed that **federal system** of government shall be adopted in India, & responsible & representative governments will be set up in provinces. This was a great achievement because the congress had suggested 'Unitary Form' of government in Nehru report. Full responsible & representative government in provinces was a good step forward for self-rule. (Secondly) the princely states also agreed to join the federation, several committees were formed to discuss different issues. The Muslims also demanded maintenance of weightage and *separate electorates*, the Hindus their abolition.

Eight subcommittees were set up to deal with the details. These committees dealt with the federal structure, provincial constitution, franchise, Sindh, the North West Frontier Province, defense services and minorities.

The conference broke up on **January 19, 1931**, and what emerged from it was a general agreement to write safeguards for minorities into the constitution and a desire to devise a *federal system* for the country. B. R. Ambedkar also demanded a separate electorate for the Untouchables.

Second Round Table Conference

The second RTC was held from *September to December 1931.* Mr. Gandhi attended as the only representative of the congress. Mr. Gandhi claimed that the Congress represented the whole of India & that there was no minority problem in the country. Muslim & other minority leaders didn't agree. Therefore, on account of Mr. Gandhi's stubborn & unfair attitude the conference couldn't achieve much but its success was that it was declared that Orissa, Sind & NWFP will be given full provincial status with governors. The minorities issue remained unresolved.

Gandhi also demanded the enforcement of *Nehru Report*, but all the minorities rejected it. During the Conference, Gandhi could not reach agreement with the Muslims on Muslim representation and safeguards. At the end of the conference Ramsay MacDonald undertook to produce a **Communal Award** for minority representation,.

Gandhi was not ready to give right of separate electorates to untouchables. He clashed with the Untouchable leader, B. R. Ambedkar, over this issue: the two eventually resolved the situation with the **Poona Pact of 1932.**

Third Round Table Conference

The third session began _on November 17, 1932_. It was short and unimportant. Only forty-six delegates attended since most of the main political figures of India were not present (included Jinnah). The Congress was once again absent, so was the Labor opposition in the British Parliament. Reports of the various committees were scrutinized. The conference ended on December 25, 1932.

The recommendations of the Round Table Conferences were included in a **White Paper**. It was published in March 1933, and debated in parliament directly afterwards, after the final reading and assent, the bill reached the Statute Book on July 24, 1935.

In this conference, **Chaudhary Rahmat** Ali, a college student, coined the name **"Pakistan"** (which means "land of pureness") as the name for the Muslim part of partitioned India. He took the "P" from Punjab, the "A" from the Afghan, the "KI" from Kashmir, the "S" from Sindh and the "TAN" from Balochistan.

SALT MARCH:

The Salt March, which took place from March to April 1930 in India, was an act of civil disobedience led by Mohandas Gandhi (1869-1948) to protest British rule in India. During the march, thousands of Indians followed Gandhi from his religious retreat near Ahmedabad to the Arabian Sea coast, a distance of some 240 miles. The march resulted in the arrest of nearly 60,000 people, including Gandhi himself.

GANDHI-IRWIN PACT:

Gandhi-Irwin Pact was an agreement signed on March 5, 1931, between Gandhi, and Lord Irwin British viceroy (1926–31) of India. It marked the end of a period of civil disobedience (*satyagraha*) in India against British rule that Gandhi and his followers had initiated with the Salt March (March–April 1930). Gandhi's arrest and imprisonment at the end of the march, for illegally making salt, sparked one of his more effective civil disobedience movements. By the end of 1930, tens of thousands of Indians were in jail (including future Indian prime minister Jawaharlal Nehru), the movement had generated worldwide publicity, and Irwin was looking for a way to end it. Gandhi was released from custody in January 1931, and the two men began negotiating the terms of the pact. In the end, Gandhi pledged to give up the *satyagraha* campaign, and Irwin agreed to release those who had been imprisoned during it and to allow Indians to make salt for domestic use. Later that year Gandhi attended the second session (September–December) of the Round Table Conference in London.

COMMUNAL AWARD:

As a result of the Second Round Table Conference, in August 1932, the then Prime Minister of Britain Ramsay Macdonald gave his 'award' known as the Communal Award. According to it, **separate representation** was to be provided for the Lower Caste, Muslims, Buddhists, Sikhs, Indian Christians and Anglo-Indians. The Untouchables were assigned a number of seats to be filled by election from special constituencies in which voters belonging to the Untouchables only could vote.

The Award was highly controversial and opposed by Mahatma Gandhi, and fasted in protest against it. Communal Award was supported by many among the minority communities, most notably the Untouchable leader, Dr. B. R. Ambedkar. After lengthy negotiations, Gandhi reached an agreement with Dr. Ambedkar to have a single Hindu electorate, with Untouchables having seats reserved within it. This is called the ***Poona Pact.*** Electorates for other religions like Muslims, Buddhists, Sikhs, Indian Christians, Anglo-Indians, Europeans remained separate.

Expected Questions & Answers

Question No. 1: why was the 2nd RTC of 1931 unsuccessful? 7 June 2000 Q.3 b

Question No. 2: The RTC of the 1930s achieved little .Give reasons why you might both agree & disagree with this statement. 14 Nov.2000 Q.3 c

Question No.3: why were the RTC held between 1930 & 1932? 7 Nov. 2001 Q.4 b

Question No. 4: how successful were the RTC of 1930-1932? Explain your answer 14 June 2005 Q.3 c

Question No. 5: the RTC of 1930 achieved more than those of 1931 & 1932. Do you agree or disagree? Give reasons for your answer. 14 June 2007 Q.3 c

Question No.6: was it necessary to hold three RTC (1930-32)? 7 June 2008 Q.3 b

Question No.7: why was the 2nd RTC of 1931 unsuccessful? 7 Nov 2009 Q.3 a

Question No.8: The First RTC of 1930 was the most successful one of all three. Do you agree or disagree? Give reasons for your answer. 14 June 2010 Q.3 c

Question No.9: Why were the three Round Table Conferences held between 1930

and 1932?7 Nov. 2011 Q.3 b

Question No.10: Was anything achieved by the Round Table Conferences of 1930 to 1932? Explain your answer14. June 2013 Q. 3 c

Question No.11: Why were three Round Table Conferences held between 1930 and 1932? 7 June 2014 Q.3

Answer to question No.4 & 10:

The round table conferences were successful to some extent because the recommendations were ultimately included in the government of India act 1935. The RTCs were held in London. The purpose was to consider the report of Simon Commission & suggest such reforms to solve the constitutional problem of India which could satisfy all people in the country. These conferences were held in London in 1930, 1931 & 1932 & all important leaders of different political parties & princes of states were invited to attend the conferences. On the whole, the Conferences were not very successful because the constitutional problem of India was not resolved but only few recommendations were acknowledged.

The first RTC held in *November 1930,*was not attended by the Congress leaders because they had put strong conditions for participating in the conference & were in jail on account of launching non-cooperation movement. However, it was agreed that federal system of government shall be adopted in India, & responsible & representative governments will be set up in provinces. This was a great achievement because the congress had suggested 'Unitary Form' of government in Nehru report. Full responsible & representative government in provinces was a good step forward for self rule. (Secondly) the princely states also agreed to join the federation, several committees were formed to discuss different issues.

The second RTC was held from *September to December 1931.* Mr. Gandhi attended as the only representative of the congress. Mr. Gandhi claimed that the Congress represented the whole of India & that there was no minority problem in the country. Muslim & other minority leaders didn't agree. Therefore, on account of Mr. Gandhi's stubborn & unfair attitude the conference couldn't achieve much but its success was that it was declared that Orissa, Sind & NWFP will be given full provincial status with governors. The minorities issue remained unresolved.

The third RTC was held in *November* **1932.** It was again not attended by the Congress. Mr. Jinnah also did not attend. This conference proved to be a formality. It broke up without achieving or agreeing to any thing of substance.

The RTCs were not successful because they failed to solve the constitutional problem of India. Congress was not satisfied because the dominion status or self rule was not granted as was promised by the Viceroy in 1930. Problem of minorities was not resolved which left the Muslims dissatisfied. Low caste Hindus also demanded separate electorate & proper representation. The new government of Britain & the new Viceroy were not in favor of giving concession to India. By and large the conferences failed to achieve anything of importance.

But the conferences were successful in the sense that some important decisions were taken

.for example federal system of government for India, representative government in provinces, separation of Sind from Bombay & full provincial status for NWFP was agreed upon. These points were including in the government of India act 1935.

Answer to question No. 3 & 6:

Since the bitter experience in war of independence 1857, the British government had adopted the policy of winning the sympathies & confidence of Indians by introducing the constitutional reforms in India. With the growing political consciousness among the Indians, the need of such reforms had become as absolute necessity.

The demand of responsible government became a controversial issue between the government & the people of India. The British government sent for the said purpose a commission headed by sir john Simon in 927. Its recommendations were rejected by congress & started civil dis obedience movement.

Nehru report in 1928 due to negation of Muslim demands failed to provide the basis of further constitutional reforms in India. Quaid's 14 points were also rejected by the Congress. Anyhow after the failure of British, Hindus & Muslims efforts to formulate such constitutional reforms, acceptable to all the elements of Indian politics, necessitated such concrete efforts which could determine the acceptable or practicable constitutional reforms in India. Besides that new labor party government was more determine to provide constitutional reforms to Indians. In pursuance of British Government policy, the viceroy enlisted the cooperation of Indian representation leaders & invited Mr. Gandhi, Mr. Jinnah, Pundit Moti Lal Nehru, Patel, Sir Tej Bahdur sapru. The congress leaders refused to participate in the meeting called by viceroy emphasizing the implementation off Nehru report before any further constitutional scheme to be discussed. However the leaders of other political parties showed great enthusiasm in the viceroy meeting. The proposed conference was held in London in three sessions, 1930, 1931 − 1932. In the following discussion we see the proceedings of London conferences known as RTC.

The Government of India Act 1935

Introduction

The **Government of India Act 1935** was passed during the "Interwar Period" and was the last pre-independent constitution of India. Government of India Act was enforced on the basis of recommendations of the Simon Commission (1927) & the reports of RTCs (1930-32)

The Act was originally passed in August 1935, and is said to have been the longest (British) Act of Parliament ever enacted by that time. Because of its length the Act was split by the Government of India Act 1935 into two separate Acts:

1. The Government of India Act 1935
2. The Government of Burma Act 1935

Key Points:

Main provisions of Government of India Act 1935 were as follows.

(i) Federal system of government will be followed with 11 provinces & all states which agreed to join it.

(ii) Principle of provincial autonomy will be followed.

(iii) Three lists of subjects were chalked out. **Central subjects** were Defense, Foreign affairs, Currency & Communication .**Provincial subjects** were education, Health, Public works & Agriculture. **Concurrent subjects** were those on which both could legislate, but central had the priority.

(iv) Central Legislature had two houses. The Upper house had 260 members & the Lower house had 375 members.

(v) Autonomy was given to all provinces. All provincial subjects were given to Indian minister who were responsible to the Legislative Assembly of the province.

(vi) **Women** for the first time were given the right to vote.

(vii) Right of separate electorate was maintained for Muslims & other communal groups.

(viii) System of Diarchy ended in the provinces & was taken to the centre.

(ix) New provinces of Orissa, Sindh & NWFP were formed & were given full provincial status.

(x) provision for the establishment of a "Federation of India", to be made up of both British India and some or all of the "princely states"

(xi) the introduction of direct elections, thus increasing the franchise from seven million to thirty-five million people

(xii) Sind was separated from Bombay

(xiii) Bihar and Orissa was split into the separate provinces

(xiv) Burma was completely separated from India .

1937 ELECTIONS:

Provincial elections were held in British India in the winter of 1936-37 as mandated by the Government of India Act 1935. Elections were held in eleven provinces - *Madras, Central Provinces, Bihar, Orissa, United Provinces, Bombay Presidency, Assam, NWFP, Bengal, Punjab and Sindh.*

The final results of the elections were declared in February 1937. The Indian National Congress emerged in power in eight of the provinces - the three exceptions being Bengal, Punjab, and Sindh. The All-India Muslim League failed to form the government in any province. The Congress ministries resigned in October and November 1939, in protest against Viceroy Lord Linlithgow's action of declaring India to be a part of the Second World War without consulting the Indian people.

The 1937 election was the first in which large masses of Indians were eligible to participate. (Approx. 30.1 million people). The results were in favour of the Indian National Congress. Of the total of 1,585 seats, it won 707 (44.6%). Among the 864 seats assigned "general" constituencies, it contested 739 and won 617. The All-India Muslim League won 106 seats (6.7% of the total), placing it as second-ranking party. The only other party to win more than 5 percent of all the assembly seats was the Unionist Party (Punjab), with 101 seats.

Expected Question & Answers:

Question No.1: why was the Govt. of India Act of 1935 so important to the future of the sub continent?
7
Nov. 2006, Q. 3 b

Question No. 2: why was there so much opposition to the government of India Act 1935? 7
Nov 2008 Q. 3 b

Question No.3: why was the Govt. of India Act of 1935 so important to the future of the sub continent?
7
June. 2011, Q. 3 b
Question No.4: Why was there so much opposition to the Government of India Act of 1935? 7

Answer to Question no. 1:

The British government was bound to introduce such constitutional scheme for India which could be practicable & acceptable to all sections of Indian society. The act of 1935 was an unusual piece of constitutional legislation & that remained a source of inspiration for the future constitutional reforms in the sub continent.

It was important to the future of the sub continent because it was the last constitutional reforms with which the British wanted to give political power in the hands of Indians.

Through this Act the federal system & parliamentary system were enforced in India. The members of Central Assembly were greatly enlarged. The number of voters was greatly increased i.e. from 6 million to 30 million & women were also allowed to vote.

Autonomy was given to all the provinces & all the ministers were to be Indians. Every province was free to formulate its programme & execute it. In other words Indians were involved in the management of the affairs of the land. New provinces of Orissa, Sindh & NWFP were created. The Act was also important because it became the basis of future constitutions of both India & Pakistan after independence; the government of Pakistan was running on the 1935 Act till 1956 when the first constitution of the country was enforced.

Topic 18

Congress Rule & Day of Deliverance 1937-39

Introduction

The Government of India Act of 1935 was practically implemented in 1937. The provincial elections were held in the winter of 1936-37. There were two major political parties in the Sub- continent at that time, the Congress and the Muslim League. Both parties did their best to persuade the masses before these elections and put before them their manifesto. The political manifestos of both parties were almost identical, although there were two major differences. Congress stood for joint electorate and the League for separate electorates; Congress wanted Hindi as official language with Deva Nagri script of writing while the League wanted Urdu with Persian script.

Congress Tyranny:

The Congress proved to be a pure Hindu party and worked during its reign only for the betterment of the Hindus. Twenty-seven months of the Congress rule were like a nightmare for the Muslims of India. Some of the Congress leaders even stated that they would take revenge from the Muslims for the last 700 years of their slavery.

After taking charge in July 1937, Congress declared Hindi as the national language and Deva Nagri as the official script. The Congress flag was given the status of national flag, slaughtering of cows was prohibited and it was made compulsory for the children to worship the picture of Gandhi at school. Band-i-Mataram, an anti-Muslim song taken from Bankim Chandra Chatterji's novel Ananda Math, was made the national anthem of the country. Religious intolerance was the order of the day. Muslims were not allowed to construct new mosques. Hindus would play drums in front of mosques when Muslims were praying.

The Congress government introduced a new educational policy in the provinces under their rule known as the Warda Taleemi Scheme. The main plan was to sway Muslim children against their ideology and to tell them that all the people living in India were Indian and thus belonged to one nation. In Bihar and C. P. the Vidya Mandar Scheme was introduced according to which Mandar education was made compulsory at elementary level. The purpose of the scheme was to obliterate the cultural traditions of the Muslims and to inculcate into the minds of Muslim children the superiority of the Hindu culture.

The Congress ministries did their best to weaken the economy of Muslims. They closed the doors of government offices for them, which was one of the main sources of income for the Muslims in the region. They also harmed Muslim trade and agriculture. When Hindu-Muslim riots broke out due to these biased policies of the Congress ministries, the government pressured the judges; decisions were made in favor of Hindus and Muslims were sent behind bars.

Expected Questions & Answer:

Question No. 1: Why was the Day of Deliverance in 1939 celebrated?   7
June 2000 Q.2 b

Question No. 2: Which of the following was the most important in the development of the Pakistan Movement.

    (i)   Jinnah's 14 points 1929

    (ii)   Govt. of India Act 1935

    (iii)   Congress Rule 1937-39.

Explain your answer with reference to all three of the above.   14
Nov. 2001 Q. 2 c

Question No. 3: why was Congress rule of 1937 -39 hated?   7
Nov. 2002 Q. 3. B

                                                                                7
Question No. 4: Why was Congress rule of 1937-39 so hated by the Muslims?
June 2004, Q. 3 b

Question No. 5: The main reason why Congress rule (1937-39) was so hated was because of the introduction of the Wardha Scheme. Do you agree?   Explain your answer.

                                                                                1

                                                                                4

Nov. 2006 Q. 3 c

Question No. 6: Why did Muslim object to the rule of the congress party between 1937-39?   7

June 2007 Q. 3 b

Question No. 6: do you agree that the celebration of the Day of Deliverance in 1939 was justified? Give reasons for your answer

14

June 2009 Q.3 c

Question No.7: The main reason why Congress rule (1937–1939) was so hated was because of the introduction of the Wardha Scheme.' Do you agree? Explain your answer. June 2012 Q.3 c

14

Question No.8: Was the main reason why Congress rule (1937–1939) was hated so much because of the introduction of Bande Matram? Explain your answer.

14

Nov. 2013 Q.3 b

Question No.9: The Government of India Act of 1935 was opposed on all sides in India. However, it was an important step towards independence, as it provided the basis for the negotiations which finally resulted in the British leaving India. Parliamentary systems had been set up, in which the Indian people gained increased representation. The 1937 elections, which both the Congress and Muslim League wanted to contest, followed quickly at provincial level.

(a) What were the outcomes of the provincial elections of 1937?   4
   May/June 2014 Q.2 a

Answer to Question No. 2:

Mr. Jinnah's 14 points 1929 were put forward in answer to Nehru report which had several points against Muslim interest .Nehru report was not acceptable to the Muslims. These points were the first ever comprehensive demand put forward by the ML. Its main aim was to protect & safeguard the rights of the Muslims of the sub- continent. At that time the Muslims had not started thinking in terms of a separate homeland & it was not included in the 14 points.

The government of India Act 1935 was a constitutional reform which gave more powers to the Indian people. It introduced provincial autonomy in provinces where all ministers were elected Indians. But the overall power remained in the hands of the British Viceroy and Governors. The congress & ML both had rejected it. The Government of India Act 1935 didn't have any effect on Pakistan movement.

There had been a series of atrocities of the Hindus against the Muslims throughout the centuries but the most horrible years for the Muslims were the years of 19 37 to 1939. These were the two years only but the congress revenge was so harsh that Muslims still feel that pain. That congress rule 1937-39 urged the Muslims to get united & strove for their separate country. That congress rule changed the psyche of the Indian Muslim leaders included Quid e Azam Pakistan became inevitable.

The Pakistan movement started after the ML passed the Lahore Resolution in March 1940 demanding a separate homeland for the Muslims. Indeed The most important factor was the Congress rule. The unbearable atrocities of the congress ministers to harm the culture, religion & the language of Muslims were difficult to be tolerated. The use of the song of the Bande Matram as national anthem hurt the Muslim feelings. Through Wardha Scheme & Vidya Mandir scheme attempts were made to propagate Hindu culture & religion. Education was to be in Hindi & Muslim Children were at a disadvantage because there was no religious education in schools.

Communal riots became a common feature in which Muslims were made victums, yet only the Muslims were blamed for initiating the riots. Ban o Cow slaughter & interruption in prayers in mosques was deliberately done. The ML prepared *'Pirpur Report'* & *'Sharif Report'* to highlight the unjust treatment to Muslims by the congress ministers. The Muslims rightly thought that it would be wrong to expect just & fair treatment from the Congress after the British left India. Therefore Muslims were compelled to ask for separate homeland & the Pakistan Movement was started.

Therefore it can be concluded that the Congress Rule 1937-39 was the most important factor in the development of Pakistan Movement.

The Pakistan resolution 1940:

Introduction

The **Lahore Resolution** (*Qarardad-e-Lahore*), commonly known as the **Pakistan Resolution** (*Qarardad-e-Pakistan*), was a formal political statement adopted by the Muslim League at the occasion of its three-day general session on 22–24 March 1940 that called for greater Muslim autonomy in British India. This has been largely interpreted as a demand for a separate Muslim state, Pakistan. The resolution was presented by **A. K. Fazlul Huq**.

Although the name "**Pakistan**" had been proposed by **Ch. Rehmat Ali** in his Pakistan Declaration in 1933, Muhammad Ali Jinnah and other leaders had kept firm their belief in Hindu-Muslim unity. However, the volatile political climate and religious hostilities gave the idea stronger backing.

Proceedings

The session was held between 22 March and 24 March 1940, at Manto Park (now Iqbal Park), Lahore. The welcome address was made by Nawab Sir Shah Nawaz Mamdot. In his speech, Jinnah recounted the contemporary situation, stressing that the problem of India was no more of an inter-communal nature, but completely an international. He criticized the Congress and endorsed the **Two-Nation Theory** and the reasons for the demand for separate Muslim homelands. According to **Stanley Wolpert,** *this was the moment when Jinnah, the former ambassador of Hindu- Muslim unity, totally transformed himself into Pakistan's great leader.*

The statement

From March 22 to March 24, 1940, the All India Muslim League held its annual session at Minto Park, Lahore. This session proved to be historical.

On the first day of the session, Quaid-i-Azam Muhammad Ali Jinnah narrated the events of the last few months. In an extempore speech he presented his own solution of the Muslim problem. To him the differences between Hindus and the Muslims were so great and so sharp that their union under one central government was full of serious risks. They belonged to two separate and distinct nations and therefore the only chance open was to allow them to have separate states.

In the words of Quaid-i-Azam: "Hindus and the Muslims belong to two different religions, philosophies, social customs and literature. They neither inter- marry nor inter-dine and, indeed, they belong to two different civilizations that are based mainly on conflicting ideas and conceptions. Their concepts on life and of life are different. It is quite clear that Hindus and Muslims derive their inspiration from different sources of history. They have different epics, different heroes and different episodes. Very often the hero of one is a foe of the other, and likewise, their victories and defeats overlap.

To yoke together two such nations under a single state, one as a numerical minority and the other as a majority, must lead to growing discontent and final destruction of any fabric that may be so built up for the government of such a state".

On the basis of the above mentioned ideas of the Quaid, A. K. Fazl-ul-Haq, the then Chief Minister of Bengal, moved the historical resolution which has since come to be known as Lahore Resolution or Pakistan Resolution.

The Resolution declared: "No constitutional plan would be workable or acceptable to the Muslims unless geographical contiguous units are demarcated into regions ....and That the areas in which the Muslims are numerically in majority as in the North-Western and Eastern zones of India should be grouped to constitute independent states in which the units shall be autonomous and sovereign".

The Resolution rejected the concept of United India and recommended the creation of an independent Muslim state consisting of Punjab, N. W. F. P., Sindh and Baluchistan in the northwest, and Bengal and Assam in the northeast. The Resolution was passed on **March 24**.

Iqbal's Allahabad Address 1930:

Several Muslim leaders and thinkers having insight into the Muslim-Hindu situation proposed the separation of Muslim India.

However, Allama Muhammad Iqbal gave the most lucid explanation of the inner feelings of Muslim community in his presidential address to the All India Muslim League at Allahabad in 1930. Allama Muhammad Iqbal was a poet, philosopher and thinker who had gained countrywide fame and recognition by 1930.

Political events had taken a complicated turn. There was a two-pronged attack on the Muslim interests. On one hand, the Hindus offered a tough opposition by proposing the **Nehru Report** as the ultimate constitution for India. On the other, the British government in India had totally ignored the Muslim demands in the **Simon Commission report.**

At this critical juncture, Iqbal realized that the peculiar problems of the Muslims in North-West India could only be understood by people belonging to this region and that in order to survive they would have to chalk out their own line of action.

In his address, *Allama Iqbal explained that Islam was the major formative factor in the life history of Indian Muslims. He defined the Muslims of India as a nation and suggested that there could be no possibility of peace in the country unless and until they were recognized as a nation. He claimed that the only way for the Muslims and Hindus to prosper in accordance with their respective cultural values was under a federal system where Muslim majority units were given the same privileges that were to be given to the Hindu majority units.*

As a permanent solution to the Muslim-Hindu problem, Iqbal proposed that Punjab, North West Frontier Province, Baluchistan and Sindh should be converted into one province. He declared that the northwestern part of the country was destined to unite as a self-governed unit, within the British Empire or without it. This, he suggested, was the only way to do away with communal riots and bring peace in the Sub-continent.

The greatest historical significance of Allama Iqbal's Allahabad address was that it cleared all political confusion from the minds of the Muslims, thus enabling them to determine their new destination. The national spirit that Iqbal fused amongst the Muslims of India later on developed into the ideological basis of Pakistan.

Expected question & answer:

Question no.1: which of the following contributed the most to the Pakistan National Movement?

    (a) Allama iqbal's address of 1930

    (b) Ch. Rehmat Ali's scheme

    (c) Mohd. Ali Jinnah's Lahore resolution of 1940?

Explain your answer with reference to all three of the above. June   14
2002 Q. 3 c

Question no.2: who was Dr. Allama Iqbal?   4
Oct/Nov 2010 Q.4 a

Question no.3: was the work of Allan Iqbal more important to the Pakistan
Movement than that of Rehmat Ali? Explain your answer.   14
June 2011 Q. 4 c

Question no.4: who was C. Rehmat Ali?   4
June 2012 Q. 3 a

Question no.5: Why was Dr Allama Iqbal an important influence on the struggle for
a separate homeland for Pakistan?   7
Oct/Nov 2014 Q. 3 b

Answer to Question No.1:

Allama iqbal gave his presidential address at the annual meeting of Muslim league held at Allahbad on **30 December 1930**. In his address he discussed the political problem of the country. He advocated the TWO NATION theory & said that Muslims in India must keep their identity. He said that the formation of a consolidated Muslim state in India was in the best interest of the Muslim of India. His address is important because it was the first occasion that the idea of a separate homeland for Muslims was given from the side of ML.

Ch. Rehmat Ali was a scholar at the Cambridge university .In **1933** he wrote a pamphlet entitled NOW OR NEVER in which he demanded that the Muslim majority provinces of NWFP , Baluchistan, Punjab, & Sindh should be grouped together to form a free Muslim state which should be named as *'Pakistan'*. But no effort was made to propagate & popularize his idea at that time. (Because it was given by a student)

The **Lahore resolution** of **March 1940** came after a bitter experience of the congress rule of 1937-39. The Muslim realized that as a policy the congress wants to abolish Muslim religion, culture & civilization. The annual meeting of ML was held in Lahore on 23 March 1940, under the president ship of Quaid-e-Azam & the Lahore resolution was passed at this meeting. In this resolution it was clearly demanded that Muslim majority provinces in the North West & eastern part of India should be grouped together to form an independent Muslim state. It was said that this would be the only workable & acceptable solution for the political problem of

India. The Lahore resolution therefore marks the real beginning of the struggle of independence of the Muslims of India.

After 1940 the demand for Pakistan became the goal & ambition of the Muslims of India. Therefore we can easily say that the Lahore Resolution contributed the most to the Pakistan National Movement.

CRIPPS MISSION 1942:

Introduction

The passing of the Pakistan Resolution was a turning point in the history of Indian Muslims; it brought about a qualitative change in their status as a minority in India. By the middle of 1940, the war had brought disaster for the allies, as France fell in June 1940, the British Government made renewed appeals for co-operation to all parties in India. In the middle of 1941, the war situation had become more serious for the allies, the **Japanese attacked Pearl Harbor** and America was involved in the war, the initial success of the Japanese armies in South-East Asia brought the war to India's doorstep.

The American President Roosevelt urged Churchill to settle matters with India that finally persuaded Churchill to send Cripps to India.

Cripps flew into Karachi on March 22, 1942, and touched down at New Delhi's airport. During his stay, Cripps met with Maulana Azad, Jinnah, Gandhi and Nehru to discuss the issues regarding India. He met Jinnah on March 25 and explained to Jinnah that he had changed his view about the Muslim League and Pakistan because of the "change in the communal feeling in India and the growth of the Pakistan movement."

Cripps publicly disclosed the contents of the Declaration at a press conference on March 29.

Contents of Cripps Mission:

(i)   An **Indian Union** would be set up with **_Dominion status_**.

(ii)   A **_Constituent Assembly_** should frame a new constitution.

(iii)   Elections for the Constituent Assembly would be held immediately after the war.

(iv)   Under the new constitution any province or state will be free to stay out of the Indian Union.

(v)   Government of India act 1935 will remain in force in the meantime.

(vi)   The C-in-C of Indian army & the finance minister will be British till the end of the war.

(vii)   These proposals will be rejected or accepted as a whole. Also these proposals will be implemented if both the congress & Muslim League accept it.

(viii)   These proposals would be applicable after the 2nd WW.

Expected Questions & Answer

Question No. 1: why did the Cripps mission fai 7

June 2002 Q. 4 b

Question No.2: why did the Cripps mission of 1942 fail? 7

Nov. 2004 Q. 3 b

Question No. 3: was the Cripps Mission in 1942 the most important factor during the 1940s that led to the partition of the Sub Continent in 1947? Give reasons for your answer. 14

Nov 2008 Q.3 c

Question No. 4: why was the Cripps mission unsuccessful? 7

June 2009 Q. 5 b

Question No. 5: why did the Cripps mission fail?

7

June 2012 Q. 3 b

Question No. 6: War broke out with Germany on 3rd September 1939 and Britain counted on the support from her Empire, including India. After the Japanese attack on Pearl Harbour, India was threatened by their advance through South East Asia. As a result the British government sent the Cripps Mission to India.

(a) Describe the Cripps Mission.

4

June 2013 Q. 3 a

Answer to question no. 3:

The *Cripps mission* was sent to India by the British government in March 1942. Its main purpose was to appease the Congress & ML because the WW II was in full fury & the British government needed full support from India. The Cripps Mission promised transfer of power after the war ended with the option that any province could opt out of the federation. The Mission also put condition that the defense of

India would be in Britain hands. The Cripps Mission was important because it made it clear that the British would have to leave India sooner or later. It also endorsed the idea & possibility of partition by giving the provinces an option to get separated. Thus the Cripps Mission laid the foundation of independence & the partition.

But besides that the Pakistan Resolution/Lahore Resolution probably remained the most important event contributed for the independence and partition of the sub-continent. Mr. Jinnah for the first time demanded a separate country for the Muslims of the Sub-continent after experiencing congress rule. He was convinced and motivated all Muslims to fight for Pakistan and within short span of seven years Independence was achieved.

Another important event was Gandhi Jinnah talks in 1944 in which Gandhi agreed to partition but argued that the British should leave India for which Hindus & Muslims should work to gather. After this the Muslim majority provinces would decide about partition through a referendum. To this Jinnah didn't agree & argued that partition should de decided before the British left. Also Jinnah wanted six provinces to be included in Pakistan, Whereas Gandhi only agreed to three. The talks failed but it became clear that Muslims will not agree to anything except partition.

The Cabinet Mission Plan (1946) was the most important event which in fact paved the way to independence & the partition. The Plan was accepted by Muslim League but the acceptance was withdrawn because the congress leaders announced that they would be free to bring any change in the plan after coming in power. The cabinet Mission also failed but it made it clear that partition was imminent & that it was the only possible solution for the Hindu – Muslim problem in India. In its ling term plan the Mission divided the provinces into three groups according to Hindu Muslim majority population & gave the option that any province or groups will be allowed to get separated. The short term plan of the Cabinet Mission to set up an interim government was accomplished after a few months of its departure. But it became clear that congress & Muslim League cannot work together & therefore the partition became unavoidable. Therefore following the announcement by Attlee that the British would leave the sub continent by 1948, the 3rd June plan was formalized.

In the conclusion it can be said that the Cripps Mission was important because it initiated the idea of partition, but the Lahore resolution was much more important because it showed the way of practical steps which could be taken towards the partition of the sub continent.

QUIT INDIA MOVEMENT BY GANDHI 1942:

The Cripps' Mission and its failure also played an important role in Gandhi's call for The Quit India Movement. In order to end the deadlock, the British government on 22nd March, 1942, sent Sir Stafford Cripps to talk terms with the Indian political parties and secure their support in Britain's war efforts. A Draft Declaration of the British Government was presented, which included terms like establishment of Dominion, establishment of a Constituent Assembly and right of the Provinces to make separate constitutions. These would be, however, granted after the cessation of the Second World War. According to the Congress this Declaration only offered India a promise that was to be fulfilled in the future. Commenting on this Gandhi said; *"It is a postdated cheque on a crashing bank."* Other factors that contributed were the threat of Japanese invasion of India, rule of terror in East Bengal and realization of the national leaders of the incapacity of the British to defend their India.

What in quit India campaign?

- May 1942 Gandhi spoke at a congress meeting in Allahabad.
- He argued that if the British left India, there would no longer be a threat of a Japanese invasion, so they should be persuaded to go by a non-violent protest.
- On 8 August 1942, the all India Congress Committee passed its Quit India Resolution, calling for an immediate withdrawal of the British.
- To support the campaign a mass struggle on nonviolent lines on the widest possible scale.
- 60,000 people arrested included Gandhi, Nehru.
- Congress party was banned.
- ML didn't approve Quit India campaign.

- Jinnah criticized the Quit India campaign as Blackmail, saying that Congress was trying to exploit British problems to win advantages for it.

Expected question & answer:

Question No. 1: why was the Quit India Movement formed in 1942? 7 June 2005, Q.4 b

Question No. 2: During the Second World War, Britain was keen to ensure that the sub-continent supported the war effort and made various promises to both the Congress Party and the Muslim League about the future of India. Following the Japanese attack on Pearl Harbour in 1941, Japan entered the war and advanced through South-East Asia as far as Burma. The British became even more anxious about the sub-continent and sent the Cripps Mission to India but it failed to resolve the situation.

(a) What was the Quit India Resolution?   4

Oct/Nov. 2013 Q. 3 a

Answer to Question No.1:

The quit India Movement was started by the Congress to gain independence by forcing the British out of India. It was a non-cooperation movement on a large scale. As a result wide spread disturbances broke out in all Hindu majority provinces.

The congress believed that the Japanese will conquer India & will liberate the country. The congress planned that if their movement synchronizes with Japanese entry into India, it would be possible for the Congress to grab power & hold the reigns of the government.

World War II was going on. During the first 2-3 years the British faced humiliating defeat at the hands of Germans & Japanese on every front. The congress was quietly jubilant over British defeat. The Japanese were running over the South East Asia without any resistance. Singapore was run over in January 1942 & soon Burma was also captured. Mr. Jinnah believed that Japan was coming to India not as India's enemy but as enemy of the British who will have to withdraw from India & India would be liberated. Congress believed that the movement should synchronize with Japanese entry into India. Congress thought that it would be a good opportunity to oust the British & take over the control of the government.

Post offices & railway were burnt & looted, telegraph wires were cut & railway track uprooted at many places. Violence resulted in many places deaths.

Congress passed a resolution on **8 August 1942** asking the British to quit India immediately & hand over the rule of India to the congress. The movement was named as Quit India movement, but the movement was suppressed & it failed. A large number of congress leaders & workers were arrested. Conditions became normal within two months.

Topic 21

THE GANDHI – JINNAH TALKS 1944:

- Gandhi was released from prison on medical grounds by the new viceroy, *Lord Wavell* in **May1944.**

- Throughout 1944 Gandhi & Jinnah met at Jinnah's house in *Bombay.*

- Gandhi wanted the League to support Congress in its struggle to remove the British while Jinnah knew that he had to secure partition before British left.

- Gandhi wanted the central government to have control over key issues such as *defense & foreign policy*, while Jinnah wanted these matters to be in the hands in the provinces.

- Gandhi considered himself to be speaking for all India while Jinnah reminded him that really he was just the spokesman of Congress.

- Gandhi gave the impression that he didn't support the *Two Nation Theory*, where as this had now become official League policy.

Expected Questions and Answer:

Question No. 1: were the Gandhi Jinnah talks the most important factor during the 1940s that led to the partition of the sub continent in 1947? Give reasons for your answer.   **14**

Nov.2005 Q. 4 c

Question No. 2: why did Gandhi Jinnah talks fail in 1944?   **7**

June 2011 Q.4 b

Answer to Question No.1:

During the period of 1940s, there were many events in the sub-continent led towards the partition and independence of the sub-continent and Gandhi Jinnah talks remained one of the important factors in this progress. Gandhi Jinnah talks were held in **Sep. 1944** at *Bombay.* Mr. Gandhi's main arguments were that All Indians are one nation because Muslims are only converts. Therefore demand of separate homeland was baseless. He believed that Congress & ML should cooperate & achieve independence first. Then a referendum may be held in Muslim majority provinces to find out if they wished to be separated. Punjab & Bengal will have to be divided because there are non.-Muslim majority districts. Defense & Foreign offices should be in control of a central authority.

Mr. Jinnah didn't agree & pressed upon an independent & sovereign Muslim state. Therefore the talks failed.

On the other hand Lahore resolution remained the most important factor for the development of independence. Lahore Resolution of March 1940 clearly demanded contiguous Muslim majority provinces in the north west & east of India should be grouped together to form an independent Muslim state . Both the Hindus & the British opposed the partition of the sub continent. But this resolution brought the Muslims of India under one banner & Pakistan became the objective, ambition & goal of the Muslim nation. The resolution increased the importance & popularity of ML. it also greatly added to the credibility & importance of Mr. Jinnah in Indian politics. ML became the true representative of the Muslims of India & Jinnah was the sole spokesman. Surprisingly great support came from the Muslims of minority provinces.

The cabinet Mission plan in March 1946 to find a solution for handing over power in India. After long negotiations the Mission gave its proposals which were accepted by ML. Congress accepted it with its own interpretations & later rejected the plan at which the ML withdrew its acceptance. The Cabinet Mission failed & went back.

Mountbatten, the new Viceroy arrived in March 1947. He realized that the demand for partition cannot be ignored & chalked out a plan for the partition of the sub continent. After getting it approved by the British government, Mountbatten announced the partition of India on **3rd June 1947**. He fixed the date of **15th August 1947** for handing over power, announced the appointment of a boundary commission & the division of assets between India & Pakistan.

Briefly speaking from all the events of 1940s the Lahore resolution was the most important factor that led to the partition of the sub continent. The resolution formed the basis of later decisions & emerged as the only proper solution for the political problem of India after the departure of the British.

LORDWAVEL &THE SIMLA CONFERENCE 1945:

In March 1944, Lord Wavell flew London to consult future policy of British Government in India.

Wavell proposed that an **Executive Council** should be set up to govern India under the present constitution, until a new constitution could be agreed on.

Wavell proposed that it would contain equal number of Muslims & Hindus & be entirely India. Apart from the viceroy & a member controlling defense.

Wavell called a conference to discuss the proposals in Simla in June 1945.

The conference had the leaders of Congress, the Muslim League, the Scheduled castes, Sikhs & other important groups.

Jinnah, liaqat Ali khan & khwaja Nazimuddin led the league delegation
.Gandhi led the congress group but president was Abul Kalam , to prove that congress was also representing Muslims.

CAUSES OF THE FAILURE OF SIMLA CONFERENCE:

Jinnah pointed that as Sikhs & scheduled castes on the council are bound to vote with Hindu, which would mean a permanent Muslim minority in council.

Jinnah also objected to the congress suggestion that it could also nominate Muslims & pointed that League had won every by – election for the last two years & was the undisputed voice of the Muslims.

Lord Wavell could see no solution so closed the conference on 14 July.

Expected questions and answers:

Question no.1: was the Simla conference of 1945 the most important factor during the 1940s leading to the partition of the Sub continent in 1947? Give reasons for your answer.   14

June 2003 Q. 3 c

Question no.2: how successful were negotiations aimed at independence during 2nd w.w? Explain your answer.   14

Oct 2010 Q.4 c

Answer to question no. 1:

Simla conference of 1945 remained one of the important factors during 1940s to the partition of the sub-continent. The Viceroy Lord Wavell called the Simla Conference in *June 1945* just at the end of WW II. The viceroy wanted to establish an Executive Council in which all subjects excepted *defense* should be given to Indians. He proposed that equal number of Hindu & Muslim members would be included in the Executive Council. For the first time the important portfolios of foreign affairs, finance & the interior would be held by Indians.The congress objected to the idea of equal number of Hindus & Muslims & desired that one Muslim seat should be given to congress because there were many Muslims in the congress party.

Quaid-e-Azam took a firm stand & explained that Muslim League being the sole representative party of Muslims of India had the right to nominate all Muslim members. The conference failed on crucial point of method of selection. But it was clear that the point of *partition of India* was not on the agenda of the Simla Conference. The Simla conference ended without achieving anything.

On the other hand Lahore resolution remained the most important factor for the development of independence. Lahore Resolution of March 1940 clearly demanded contiguous Muslim majority provinces in the north west & east of India should be grouped together to form an independent Muslim state . Both the Hindus & the British opposed the partition of the sub-continent. But this resolution brought the Muslims of India under one banner & Pakistan became the objective, ambition & goal of the Muslim nation. The resolution increased the importance & popularity of ML. it also greatly added to the credibility & importance of Mr. Jinnah in Indian politics. ML became the true representative of the Muslims of India & Jinnah was the sole spokesman. Surprisingly great support came from the Muslims of minority provinces.

The cabinet Mission plan in March 1946 to find a solution for handing over power in India. After long negotiations the Mission gave its proposals which were accepted by ML. Congress accepted it with its own interpretations &

later rejected the plan at which the ML withdrew its acceptance. The Cabinet Mission failed & went back. Mountbatten, the new Viceroy arrived in March 1947. He realized that the demand for partition cannot be ignored & chalked out a plan for the partition of the sub-continent. After getting it approved by the British government, Mountbatten announced the partition of India on 3rd June 1947. He fixed the date of 15th August 1947 for handing over power, announced the appointment of a boundary commission & the division of assets between India & Pakistan.

Briefly speaking from all the events of 1940s the Lahore resolution was the most important factor that led to the partition of the sub-continent. The resolution formed the basis of later decisions &

emerged as the only proper solution for the political problem of India after the departure of the British.

GENERALELECTIONS1945-1946

After the failure of Simla conference Lord Wavell announced general and provincial elections after which constitutional making body was to be set up. Both parties launched election campaigns. Because they knew that the elections were essential for the future of India, as the results were to play an important role in determining their standing.

The League wanted to sweep the Muslim constituencies so as to prove that they were the sole representatives of the Muslims of India, while on the other hand Congress wanted to prove that they represent all Indians. Both parties raised different slogans during whole election campaign. Congress tried to get support of all those parties who were against the Muslim League.

Elections for central legislature were held on December 1945 with the limited franchise. During these elections Congress won about 80 percent of the general seats and 91.3 percent general votes and Muslim League won all 30 reserved seats for Muslims. Provincial election held on 1946 results was not different. Muslim League won 95 percent seats for Muslims and Congress won all seats for non-Muslims.

CABINET MISSION PLAN 1946

- In March 1946, a three man delegation including Lord Pethic Lawrence (secretary of state for India) sir Stafford Cripps (president of the board of trade) and A.V Alexander (first lord of the admiralty) was sent to India to try to find a settlement acceptable to all.
- They arrived in New Delhi on 24 March 1946.
- The cabinet mission proposed that an interim government should be set up & the government would form an All-India commission from members of the provincial & central legislatures.
- In 1946 the cabinet mission announced its final plan.

Proposals of the cabinet mission plan:

- It rejected the idea of establishing Pakistan.
- Three different parts suggested to a post British India.

(a)   The Hindu majority territories.

(b)   The western Muslim population

(c)   Bengal & Assam

- Each part would have its local autonomy & would be able to draw up its new constitution.
- Foreign affairs, defense & communication would be managed by a central Indian union.
- League stated that it was ready to nominate members to an interim cabinet to oversee the move to independence by this plan.
- Nehru said that congress would not feel bounded by the plan after British left so the plan dropped.

DIRECT ACTION DAY 1946

Direct Action Day, also known as the **Great Calcutta Riot**, was on 16 August 1946—a day of widespread riot and manslaughter in the city of Calcutta (now known as Kolkata) in the Bengal province of British India. The day also marked the start of what is known as **"The Week of the Long Knives".**

The protest triggered massive riots in Calcutta, instigated by the Muslim League and its Volunteer Corps against Hindus and Sikhs, followed by retaliatory attacks on Muslims by Congress followers and supporters. In Calcutta, within 72 hours, more than **4,000 people** lost their lives and 100,000 residents in the city of Calcutta were left homeless. Violence in Calcutta sparked off further religious riots in the surrounding regions of Noakhali, Bihar, United Province (modern Uttar Pradesh), Punjab, and the North Western Frontier Province. These events sowed the seeds for the eventual Partition of India.

THE 3RD JUNE PLAN 1947

When all of Mountbatten's efforts to keep India united failed, he asked Ismay to chalk out a plan for the transfer of power and the division of the country. It was decided that none of the Indian parties would view it before the plan was finalized.

The plan was finalized in the Governor's Conference in April 1947, and was then sent to Britain in May where the British Government approved it.

However, before the announcement of the plan, Nehru who was staying with Mountbatten as a guest in his residence at Simla, had a look at the plan and rejected it. Mountbatten then asked V. P. Menon, the only Indian in his personal staff, to present a new plan for the transfer of power. Nehru edited **Menon's formula** and then Mountbatten himself took the new plan to London, where he got it approved without any alteration. Attlee and his cabinet gave the approval in a meeting that lasted not more than five minutes. In this way, the plan that was to decide the future of the Indo-Pak Sub-continent was actually authored by a Congress-minded Hindu and was approved by Nehru himself.

Mountbatten came back from London on May 31, and on June 2 met seven Indian leaders. These were Nehru, Patel, Kriplalani, Quaid-i-Azam, Liaquat, Nishtar and Baldev Singh. After these leaders approved the plan, Mountbatten discussed it with Gandhi and convinced him that it was the best plan under the circumstances. The plan was made public on June 3, and is thus known as the June 3rd Plan.

Proposals of the 3rd June plan;

- Two states should be set up India & Pakistan.
- The interim government of both states was the 1935 government of India act.
- Each state was to have dominion status & have an executive responsible to a constituent assembly.
- Muslim majority provinces would vote either to stay in India or join Pakistan. In Sindh & Baluchistan, provincial Legislatures voted to join Pakistan. Bengal & Punjab decided that they should join Pakistan but their Muslim – minority areas will remain in India. NWFP also joined Pakistan after holding a referendum. The Muslim-majority district of Sylhet in Assam joined the eastern wing of Pakistan.

(a) Day after a 3rd June plan, Mountbatten said that final transfer of Power might be brought forward from June 1948 to 15 August 1947.

(b) On 15 July 1947 the independence Act was passed.

(c) From 15 august British India would be partitioned into two Dominion states.

THE RADCLIFFE BOUNDARY AWARD 1947:

- SIR Cyril Radcliff was appointed to head a Boundary Commission to establish new borders.

- Radcliff had four assistants, two nominated by the league & two by the congress.
- The decision of the Boundary Commission known as "the Boundary Award or Radcliff Award" was announced on 16 August 1947.
- Calcutta, Gurdaspur, Ferozpur were awarded to India though they were Muslim majority areas.
- Jinnah told people of Pakistan that the awards were wrong, unjust & perverse.

SECTION III

ACHIEVEMENT OF QUAID-E-AZAM

As a leader:

- He was the 1st governor general of Pakistan.
- He was an inspiration for the nation.
- He took the role of Chief Executive in the new government & chaired the cabinet meetings.
- He was the president of the constituent assembly.

Building a Nation:

- Jinnah dealt with the problems faced by Pakistan at the time of partition.
- Country was divided into east & West Pakistan & he coup with the geographical problems as well.
- Jnnah stressed everyone to work together to create nation.
- He said: "every one of us should think, feel & act as Pakistani & we all should be proud on being Pakistanis alone.
- Jinnah was opposed to religious intolerance, provincialism & racialism.
- He called himself as the protector general of religious minorities.
- He was determined to see Pakistan a land of tolerance.
- He said that Islamic ideas about justice & equality demanded that any non Muslim who was to remain in Pakistan should be treated fairly.
- Jinnah helped refugees by setting up a relief fund to rehabilitate them.
- He secured the membership of the country to UNO in September 1947.

Building a government:

- Quaid knew that no problem could be solved until the country had an administration that could take decision about the problems.
- Liaqat ali khan was made the prime minister & a cabinet was formed. A constituent assembly was also set up.
- Karachi became the capital of Pakistan.

- Central secretariat was setup to run the country.
- Civil service was reorganized & civil rules were drafted.
- Quaid was determined that government officials should have right attitude to their work.
- He informed the officials that they were the servants of people & not the rulers of the country. He wanted them to work with national spirit.

Building an economy:

- Pakistan was denied its full share of wealth.

- It was difficult to convert Pakistan from an agricultural country to one with a degree of industrial development.
- On 1st July 1948, Quaid established State bank of Pakistan to help develop the economy.
- Quaid reached a compromise with India in the canal water dispute, which ensured that Pakistan's Agriculture would not be denied precious water supplies.
- He also urged to set up industries in Pakistan.

Establishing national security:

- Pakistan had been given poor military equipment & it lacked senior cadre officers for army.
- Army needed more officers.
- Quaid didn't want Pakistan become a military oligarchy.

Conclusion:
- Quaid died on 11 September 1948.
- Times news paper wrote. *"No succeeding GG can quite fill his place as the Father of the Nation"*.
- Stanley Walport said, **"Few *individuals significantly alter the course of history, still very few change the map of the world, hardly anyone can be credited with creating a nation state, Mohammad Ali Jinnah did three"*.**

Expected questions:

Question No. 1: which of the following contributed the most to the establishment of a separate homeland for Muslims.

    (i)   Gandhi Jinnah talks 1944

    (ii)   Simla conference 1945

    (iii)   Cabinet mission plan 1946

Explain your answer with reference to all three of the above.   14

Nov 2002, Q.3 c

Question No. 2: How important was Mohammad Ali Jinnah to the Pakistan movement? Explain your answer. 14

Nov 2001. Q. 3 c

Question No. 3: what was the Direct Action Day? 4

June 2010 Q.3 a

INITIAL PROBLEMS OF PAKISTAN 1947 -48:

Introduction:

- Quaid-e-azam sworn as the Governor General of Pakistan on 14 august 1947.
- He said **"Pakistan has come to exist for ever".**

Geographical problems:

Pakistan was **split** into two separate parts almost a **thousand miles** apart. East Pakistan comprised of most of Bengal and the Sylhet which voted in a referendum to join Pakistan. West Pakistan comprised of west Punjab, Sindh, Baluchistan and the NWFP. The princely states of Dir, Swat, Chitral, Amb, Hunza, Gilgit and Bahawalpur also joined Pakistan. These two wings of Pakistan were separated by about a 1000 miles of land that belonged to India. There was nothing common between these two wings except religion.

Political problems:

India inherited government buildings, furnishings even officials from the British. Pakistan had none of these. India had officials, members of the Indian national congress, with political experience to take over the government. In Pakistan, the constituent Assembly members were mostly wealthy landlords with little political experience. Pakistan lacked both the administrative and the government machinery to run the affairs of a new country Quaid-e-azam would need to find a capital, a government and officials to ensure the efficient government of the new state. Perhaps the major problem was that the Quaid-e-azam had suffered from **tuberculosis.**

Economic problems:

Pakistan was underdeveloped with very little industry. Only **Karachi** had the modern port but much of Pakistan had no linked to the industrialization that had taken place in central India. Around 90 % people lived in the country side and only 8 towns had a population of 100,000.Pakistan's agriculture didn't produce enough of a surplus to create the wealth needed for industrialization. Only jute export produced the major source of foreign exchange earnings for Pakistan but the problems created by partition are exemplified by the fact that in

1947 Pakistan didn't have a single jute mill. All the jute mills were in the new India.

The percentage of economic assets in Pakistan after partition:

- Industrial enterprises: 10 %

- Industrial workers : 6.5 %

- Electrical capacity : 5%

- Mineral deposits : 10 %

Electricity Problem

Due to transfer of Muslim majority areas to India and unfair demarcation, electricity system of West Punjab was disrupted ,because all power stations were at Mundi, a predominantly Muslim majority area, gifted to India but Quiad-e-Azam said:

"If we are to exist as a nation ,we will have to face the problems with determination and force."

Social problems:

Pakistan was mainly made up of 5 different regions. Some historians have gone as far as suggesting that really it was 5 different nations. Certainly there were five different population groupings.

(i)   the Pakhtuns in the north

(ii)   the Balochs in the west

(iii)   the Sindhis in the south

(iv)   the Punjabis in the north east

(v)   the Bengalis in the east

These people had different traditions, cultures, languages and lifestyles. Baluchistan and Bengal in 1947 were not completely sure that they now wanted to transfer allegiance to a new Pakistan, where once again the official language Urdu would not be the one they spoke.

The accession of the princely states:

Lord Mountbatten gave the right to 462 princely states to choose between India and Pakistan. Their location and their religion made the choice a straightforward one. In 1947 the northern areas of Dir, Swat, Chitral, Amb and Hunza joined Pakistan. Bahawalpur also joined Pakistan; Sylhet in East also joined Pakistan through referendum.

Hyderabad

It was the largest of the princely states with a population of 160 million. It was wealthy with revenue of 160 million rupees. Nizam wanted to join Pakistan but he was pressurized to join India due to non-Muslim population there. In august he filed a complaint before UNO. But before it could be heard Indian troops captured Hyderabad.

Junagarh

it was a small state on the coast, 300 miles south of Karachi. Its prince was Muslim but population was non-Muslim. Prince announced to join Pakistan in 1947.But Lord Mountbatten informed Pakistan that the accession of *Junagarh was an encroachment on Indian sovereignty and territory.* Ultimately Indian troops surrounded the state and took the control. Pakistan protested to the UNO about the illegal occupation but the matter remains unresolved.

The Kashmir Issue:

The most serious disagreement between India and Pakistan concerned the state of Jammu and Kashmir. Its boundaries with Tibet, China, Afghanistan and Russia gave it great strategic importance. Most of the 4 million inhabitants of Kashmir were Muslims but the maharaja was Hindu. In September 1947 he started a campaign to drive many Muslims out of Kashmir. Over 200,000 fled to Pakistan and finally the Muslims rose in rebellion. The Maharaja was forced to turn to India for help to crush the Muslims. Indian help came and the Maharaja Hari Singh agreed to accede to India. Pakistan also sent troops to help Kashmir (Muslims).Neither side was strong enough for a long war. So in January 1948 the matter referred to the UNO.A ceasefire was arranged on Jan. 1949 and Kashmir was divided between India and Pakistan. India retained the largest area of Kashmir including the capital Srinagar. Indian Prime Minister Nehru agreed that a referendum would be held in Kashmir to determine the wishes of the people, *once the situation has normalized.* This referendum has not been held yet...

The division of financial and military assets:

It was agreed that the assets were to be divided on the ratio of 17 to India and 5 to Pakistan. This reflected the relative size and populations of the country. In June 1947 it was agreed that Pakistan would be paid **750 million** rupees of the **4 billion** rupees in the reserve bank. First 200 million rupees were paid but later on India refused to pay the rest saying Pakistan would only use it to buy arms to fight against India. Gandhi was determined that the division of assets should be fair and took steps to persuade India to pay the due money. He used the threat of a hunger strike and successfully persuaded the Indian government to pay a further 500 million rupees. Armed forces and the military equipment were split 36 % to 64% between Pakistan and India.

The armed forces personnel were given freedom to opt for whichever country they wanted. Muslim regiments went to Pakistan and non- Muslim to India. Pakistan's army comprising on **150,000 men** and had only 2500 trained Muslim officers. It required 4000 officers; ultimately Jinnah had to hire 500 British officers temporarily. All **16 ordinance** factories were in India, and it refused to hand over any. Pakistan had no factory for making military goods. Eventually India agreed to pay 60 million rupees in lieu of handing over ordnance factories. The military supplies which India agreed to hand over were often old, worn, damaged and obsolete.

The canal water dispute:

The canal water dispute had its origin in the partition of Punjab in 1947.West Pakistan relies upon irrigation from a series of canals which draw water from the 3 main rivers in the area, the Indus, the Jhelum, and the Chenab. The problem for Pakistan was that the flow of water was controlled at a series of 'headwork's' lay in the part of east Punjab (India).Soon India and Pakistan indulge into a canal water dispute. Pakistan called for the matter to be settled by international court of justice but India refused. In May 1948 a temporary agreement was reached and India agreed to allow water from east Punjab to flow into west Punjab.

Refugees and the accommodation crises:

In the years immediately before partition there was widespread violence between Muslims and the non- Muslims communities across India. The summer of 1947 saw rioting which led to numerous deaths. When the **boundary Award** was announced in august 1947 things became worse. Millions of people found themselves living in the wrong country and became victims of communal attacks. That year witnessed the largest migration of mankind and also some of the worst scenes of communal violence. Over 20 million people had moved from India to Pakistan or in other direction by Jan. 1948.Many Muslim historians believe that Hindus and Sikhs had an organized programme for the massacre of Muslim refugees. A million men, women and children died as a result of the violence or the rigors of the long journey. Nearly 10 million people were made homeless. Karachi alone received nearly 2 million refugees in 1947.That was impossible for Pakistan to provide accommodations to that mass number of people. In September 1947 the authorities in Delhi had to declare martial law as non-Muslim refugees had begun a slaughter of local Muslims. India and Pakistan were so concerned about the communal violence that they began to cooperate in trying to control it.

Drawbacks in Educational System:

Lack of proper planning:

There is no proper planning. Planning needs correct facts and figures which are not available. Innovations are neither research based nor are introduced after proper preparation. They are introduced with a stroke of pen, and are cancelled ill equal haste. Nationalization and de-nationalization of schools , semester system and its cancellation, comprehensive schools, superior science colleges are examples.

Policies and their implementation:

Education policies are framed, but are not fully implemented with honesty and whole heartedness. Five policies were framed, the latest was in 1979. Over 1000 recommendations were made but only 25% were implemented. A new policy is introduced with every change of government.

Administrative set up:

Officers at high level want to have all powers in their hands. At lower level there is lack of proper supervision and control.

Lack of funds:

This is the most important draw back. The government has no money to open more primary schools to accommodate all children of school going age. The result is that there is overcrowding in primary and secondary schools. Most of the money allocated to education is spent on salaries. There is no money for research, development or teachers' training.

Poor condition of Schools:

School buildings are in bad shape. Buildings are neglected and dilapidated. There are thousands of schools without proper class rooms. There is no proper furniture or facilities of drinking water, toilets or playing grounds. Very often classes are held under the open sky and children are sitting on bare ground.

Teachers:

In Pakistan teachers are a neglected community. No incentive is provided by the governments or the society to the teachers and they are considered to be a community known for their intellectual and economic backwardness. Training of teachers is also on old and out-moded lines and it does not conform with the latest methods and trends.

Examination System:

Examination system is in primitive state. The system is based on selective study, memorizing the text books or notes is all what is required. Memorization of a narrow range of predictable topics is rewarded by high marks. The system of examination is counter-productive as far as intellectual growth is concerned. It tempts the students to cram rather than analyse and apply the knowledge to solve problems.

Expected questions:

Question No. 1: Explain three reasons for the canal water dispute between India and Pakistan.

(7)   **June 2000 Q. 4 b**

Question No. 2: how successful did India and Pakistan handle the Kashmir issue up to 1988? Explain your answer. (14)   Nov. 2000 Q. 4 c

Question No.3: why was Pakistan faced with a refugee problem in 1947? (7)   Nov. 2000 Q.4 b

Question No. 4: How successful was the government of Pakistan in solving the problems of partition during 1947 and 1948? Explain your answer.   (14)   June 2002 Q.4.c

Question No. 5: why did Pakistan join the UN in 1947? (7)   Nov. 2002 Q.5 b

Question No. 6: why was the division of the armed forces and military assets a problem for Pakistan in 1947? (7)   Nov. 2003 Q. 4 b

Question No. 7: was the refugee issue the most important problem facing the newly formed government of Pakistan in 1947? Give reasons for your answer. (14)   June 2004 Q. 3 c

Question No. 8: how successful did India and Pakistan handle the Kashmir issue between 1947 and 1988? Explain your answer. (14)   Nov. 2004 Q. 4c

Question No.9: why did Pakistan face so many problems in the provision of education between 1947 and 1988? (7)   Nov. 2004 Q.5 b

Question No. 10: The government of Pakistan was totally successful in solving the problems of partition during 1947 and 1948. Do you agree? Explain your answer. (14)   June 2005 Q. 4 c

Question No. 11: how successful did India and Pakistan handle the Kashmir issue between 1946 and 1988? Explain your answer. (14)   Nov. 2006 Q. 4 c

Question No.12: Why was Pakistan faced with a refugee problem in 1947? (7)   Nov. 2006 Q. 4 b

Question No.13: why did Pakistan join the UN in 1947? (7)   June 2007 Q. 4 b

Question No. 14: The canal water dispute was the most important problem facing the newly established government of Pakistan in 1947. do you agree or disagree? Give reasons for your answer. (14)   June 2007 Q.4c

Question No.15: why did educational reform become such an important issue between 1947 and 1988? (7)   Nov 2007 Q.4 b

Question No. 16: the low rate of literacy was the most important social problem facing Pakistan between 1947 and 1988. do you agree? Give reasons for your answer. (14)   June 2008 Q.4 c

Question No.17: the formation of a government was the most important problem facing the newly established country of Pakistan in 1947, do you agree? (14)   Nov 2009

Q.4 c

Question No.18: what was the Canal Water Dispute? (4)   June 2010 Q.4a

Question No.19: why did Pakistan join the UN in 1947? (7)   June 2010 Q.4 b

Question No. 20: Describe the refugee problem. (4)   No. 2012 Q.4.a

Question No.21: The government of Pak. Was totally successful in solving the problems of partition during 1947 and 1948. Do you agree? Explain your answer. (14)   June 2012 Q. 4

c

ANSWER TO QUESTION NO. 4:-

The government of Pakistan was successful to some extent in solving the problems of partition during 1947 and 1948.When Pakistan came into existence in August 1947, it faced many difficulties. The most important problem was the formation of a central government of Pakistan. There were no offices, no office equipment and no office workers. The central government offices were set up in army barracks and hired residential buildings. However under the guidance of Quaid –e–Azam and with courage and confidence, the difficulties were overcome and the government of Pakistan started functioning smoothly. Quaid – e – Azam and Liaqat Ali Khan became the Governor general and Prime Minister respectively.

The problem of refugees was a very big problem. Communal riots had started in Indian Punjab and Delhi. Millions of Muslims had the leave their homes and had to run to Pakistan. The Pakistan government set up camps for the refugees and looked after them for several months. They were gradually settled in the new country. Under the guidance of Quaid-e- Azam a new department was created for rehabilitation of the refugees.

The division of military assets was another problem. The division was to be made at a ratio of 36:64 between the two countries. Bu since all big military stores was on the side of India. The equipment given to Pakistan was obsolete and consisted of unusable machinery and equipment. Pakistan had to suffer a great loss and had to start from a scratch. In the division of financial assets again the Indian leaders showed great dishonesty and unfairness. The payment was not only withheld for a long time, But out of a sum of Rs: 750 million only Rs: 700 million were paid in several instalments. Rs: 50 million were never paid at all.

Canal water dispute also arose in April 1948 when India stopped the supply of water in the canals coming out or River Ravi and River Sutlej, because their head-works were located in India. A large agricultural area of Pakistan was badly affected. After lengthy negotiations this problem was solved with the cooperation of World Bank under the Indus Water Treaty in 1960.The accession of three princely states of Junagarh, Hyderabad and Kashmir created great problems for Pakistan. The ruler of Junagarh formally acceded to Pakistan. But the population was mostly non-Muslim; therefore, India occupied the state with the help of armed forces. The state of Hyderabad wanted to remain independent. But in September 1948, the Indian army forcibly occupied the state. Kashmir had an overwhelmingly Muslim majority population. But the Hindu Maharaja formally acceded to India against the wishes of the people. India airlifted her troops and occupied the state capital Srinagar. Kashmir still remains a disputed territory. India does not obey the resolutions of the Security Council which has ordered a free and fair plebiscite in Kashmir. Four wars have been fought between India and Pakistan and two agreements were finalized, but the problem of Kashmir remains unsolved mainly because of unfair and stubborn attitude of India.

Besides all these uncertainty Pakistan was successful in overcoming its initial problem.

TOPIC 25

Early years 1947 to 1958:

Liaqat Ali khan

Liaquat Ali Khan's contributions to the struggle for independence were numerous. After independence, he was thus the natural choice for the premiership. Liaquat Ali Khan was appointed as the first Prime Minister of Pakistan.

Being the first Prime Minister of the country, Liaquat Ali Khan had to deal with a number of difficulties that Pakistan faced in its early days. He helped Quaid-i-Azam in solving the riots and refugee problem and in setting up an effective administrative system for the country. He established the groundwork for Pakistan's foreign policy. He also took steps towards the formulation of the constitution.

Objectives Resolution

He presented The **Objectives Resolution,** a prelude to future constitutions, in the Legislative Assembly. The house passed it on March 12, 1949. It is considered to be the "Magna Carta" in Pakistan's constitutional history. Liaquat Ali Khan called it "the most important occasion in the life of this country, next in importance, only to the achievement of independence". Under his leadership a team also drafted the first report of the Basic Principle Committee and work began on the second report.

During his tenure, India and Pakistan agreed to resolve the dispute of Kashmir in a peaceful manner through the efforts of the United Nations. According to this agreement a ceasefire was affected in Kashmir in January 1948. It was decided that a free and impartial plebiscite would be held under the supervision of the UN.

After the death of Quaid-i-Azam, he tried to fill the vacuum created by the departure of the Father of the Nation. The problem of religious minorities flared during late 1949 and early 1950, and it seemed as if India and Pakistan were about to fight their second war in the first three years of their independence.

Liaquat- Nehru Pact

At this critical moment in the history of South Asia, Prime Minister Liaquat Ali Khan met Nehru to sign the *Liaquat- Nehru Pact in 1950.* The Liaquat-Nehru Pact was an effort on his part to improve relations and reduce tension between India and Pakistan. In May 1951, he **visited the United States** and set the course of Pakistan's foreign policy towards closer ties with the West. An important event during his premiership was the establishment of *National Bank of Pakistan* in November 1949, and the installation of a paper currency mill in Karachi.

Assassination

Liaquat Ali Khan was unfortunately assassinated on *October 16, 1951*. Security forces immediately shot the assassin, who was later identified as *Syed Akbar*. The question of who was behind his murder is yet to be answered. The government officially gave Liaquat Ali Khan the title of *Shaheed-i-Millat.*

Khawaja Nazimuddin

After Pakistan came into being on August 14, 1947, **Nazimuddin** was appointed the first Chief Minister of the Province of East Bengal. When the founder of Pakistan, Quaid-i-Azam Muhammad Ali Jinnah died on September 11, 1948, Nazimuddin was appointed as the second Governor General of Pakistan and later on after the assassination of Liaqat Ali Khan Nazimuddian became the second Prime Minister of Pakistan. Malik Ghulam Mohammad took the office of G.G. The movement for *Tahaffuz-i-Khatam-i-Nabuwat* and the worsening food condition in Punjab caused a lot of trouble for Khawaja Nazimuddin and this led to his dismissal on 17 April 1953.

After the dismissal of Khawaja Nazimuddin, the **Governor General Malik Ghulam Mohammad** appointed

Muhammad Ali Bogra,

He was from East Pakistan, as the Prime Minister. Malik Ghulam Muhammad was forced to retire from the post of Governor General due to his failing health and

Major General Iskander Mirza, the Minister of Interior, took over the office. Although the expulsion of

Ghulam Muhammad from power seemed necessary, yet his successor, Iskander Mirza proved to be a greater menace for the country.

It was during the tenure of Muhammad Ali Bogra that Pakistan joined *C. E. N. T. O.* and *S. E. A. T. O.* Governor General also dismissed Muhammad Ali Bogra on August 8, 1955.

Bogra's constitutional proposal, known as the **Bogra Formula,** was presented before the Constituent Assembly of Pakistan on October 7, 1953. The plan proposed for a Bicameral Legislature with equal representation for all the five provinces of the country in the Upper House. A total of 50 seats were reserved for the Upper House. The 300 seats for the Lower House were to be allocated to the provinces on the basis of proportionate representation.

Chaudhry Muhammad Ali was appointed as the new Prime Minister on August 11, 1955. But soon Chaudhry Muhammad Ali had to resign as a Prime Minister under unfavourable political circumstances on September 8, 1956, it was during his tenure that Chaudhry Muhammad Ali presented the 1956 Constitution and **Iskander Mirza** was elected the first President of Pakistan.

Iskander Mirza
He was sworn-in as the **first President** under the 1956 Constitution. During his regime not only was the first Constitution of Pakistan finalized, but also all the provinces and princely states of West Pakistan were knitted together to form **One Unit** of the West Pakistan Province.

During his tenure from 1956 to 1958, President **Iskander Mirza** brought about various cabinet changes and advocated a controlled democracy for Pakistan. **Muhammad Ali Bogra** was the first Prime Minster under Iskander Mirza. Bogra could not stay at this position for long; he resigned and went back to the U. S. A. where he was reinstated as the Ambassador of Pakistan.

After Bogra, **Chaudhry Muhammad Ali** became the next Prime Minster. It was under his premiership that the establishment of One Unit was given practical shape and the Constitution of 1956 was introduced. *Huseyn Shaheed Suhrawardy, I. I. Chundrigar and Malik Feroz Khan Noon* succeeded him as Prime Ministers under Iskander Mirza's despotic rule.

Due to severe political instability and continuous replacing of premiership, President Iskander Mirza turned towards General Ayub Khan, the Commander-in-Chief of the armed forces of

Pakistan. At midnight between October 7 and 8, 1958, the President of Pakistan abrogated the Constitution and imposed Martial Law in the country. This brought an end to the term of Malik Feroz Khan Noon, which lasted for less than a year. The Parliamentary Government came to an end in Pakistan, thus setting the stage for the recurrence of Martial Law again and again in the future.

In collusion with the Commander-in-Chief, Muhammad Ayub Khan, Iskander Mirza abrogated the Constitution on October 7, 1958 and declared Martial Law. Iskander Mirza and Ayub Khan began the new era with apparent unanimity. Although the two were responsible for bringing about the change, they had different views on dealing with the new situation. Share of power soon led to a struggle between the two, which ended with Iskander Mirza being arrested and exiled to Britain where he later died.

OBJECTIVE RESOLUTION 1949:

On March 12, 1949, the Constituent Assembly adopted a resolution moved by Liaquat Ali Khan, the then Prime Minister of Pakistan. It was called the Objectives Resolution. It proclaimed that the future constitution of Pakistan would not be modelled on European pattern, but on the ideology and democratic faith of Islam.

The Objectives Resolution, proclaimed the following principles:

1. Sovereignty belongs to Allah alone.

2. The State shall exercise its powers and authority through the chosen representatives of the people.

3. The principles of democracy, freedom, equality, tolerance and social justice, as enunciated by Islam, shall be fully observed.

4. Muslims shall be enabled to order their lives in the individual and collective spheres in accordance with the teachings of Islam as set out in the Holy Quran and Sunnah.

5. Adequate provision shall be made for the minorities to freely profess and practice their religions and develop their cultures.

6. Pakistan shall be a federation.

7. Fundamental rights shall be guaranteed.

8. Judiciary shall be independent.

The Objectives Resolution is one of the most important and illuminating documents in the constitutional history of Pakistan. The importance of this document lies in the fact that it combines the good features of Western and Islamic democracy. It is a happy blend of modernism and Islam.

Public and Representative Officer's disqualification Act (PRODA):

- It was an act for debarring of a government officer from public office for a suitable period of time if he is judicially found guilty of misconduct in public office or any representative capacity in any matter.
- By this Act complaints could be made to the G.G or provincial Governors who could order an enquiry by judges.
- Anyone found guilty under PRODA was debarred from office.
- The law was designed to eliminate corruption.

One unit policy:

- In November 1954, M. Ali Bogra had proposed that the 4 provinces and 10 princely states within Pakistan should be joined together to form West Pakistan.

- On 5th Oct 1955 Mirza Ghulam Mohammad passed an order unifying all of West Pakistan in what became known as One Unit Scheme.

M.Ali Bogra said: "There *will be no Bengalis, no Punjabis, no Sindhis, no Pathans, no Balochis, no Bahawalpuris, and no Khairpuris. The disappearance of these groups will strengthen the integrity of Pakistan*".

Expected Questions
Q. 1: why was it so difficult to agree on a new constitution in 1950? Nov. 2011 Q. 4 b
Q.2: Describe the constitutional crises of 1954-55. June 2012 Q. 4 a

Field Marshal Mohammad Ayub Khan 1958 to 1969

- Born in 14 May 1907
- Son of a Risal Dar Major Mir daad Khan
- Read in Aligarh College.
- Joined Indian Army in 1926
- Ayub khan announced that he hoped that a period of military rule would settle Pakistan.

POLITICAL AND CONSTITUTIONAL REFORMS:

1959 Basic Democracies:

- The first step in Ayub Khan's constitutional reforms came with the introduction of the Basic
  Democracies order on **26 Oct. 1959.**
- That was 4 tier systems in which ordinary people elected **union council** members, who in turn elected **district** and **divisional** members.
- Later it was stated in the 1962 constitution that the 80,000 elected Basic Democrats would also form the Electoral College for the election of the **president** and members of the central and provincial legislatures.
- At the end of 1959, Ayub asked the basic democrats for a vote of confidence in him and **on 17 Feb. 1960** he was confirmed as president.
- He then announced the creation of a constitution commission to make recommendations for a new constitution.

The 1962 Constitution:

- The new constitution was announced on **1 March 1962.**
- Ayub described it as combining *"democracy with discipline"*.
- In reality it set up a presidential form of government.

It stated that:
  (i)   The president could be removed unless impeached.

(ii)	The president nominated the cabinet from the members of the national assembly.
(iii)	The president nominated the heads of the judiciary and the provincial governors.
(iv)	The national legislatures could not pass a law without the approval of the president.
(v)	Both Urdu and Bengali were recognized as two of the national languages.
(vi)	The national assembly session was to be held in both Dhaka and Islamabad.
(vii)	If the president were from West Pakistan then the speaker of the national assembly was to be from East Pakistan.

- The new constitution was introduced without debate and Ayub brought Martial law to an end soon afterwards.
- The new National assembly met for the first time on **8 June 1962.**
- The first act was to remove the ban on political parties.
- Ayub's reforms had increased the powers of the ruling elite.

- Major landlords dominated the elections.
- The constitution also further upset the people of East Pakistan.
- They felt that the Pakistan's government was in the hands of military and civil officials from West Pakistan.

Election of 1965:

- In **Jan 1965** elections were held for the presidency.
- Ayub khan was nominated by a new party , the *Convention Muslim League*
- He believed that the opposition parties were too divided to put up a credible opponent in the elections.
- He was however wrong, the opposition parties all agreed to support the sister and advisor of the Quaid, *Mohtarma Fatima Jinnah.*
- In the election Ayub Khan won **64 %** of the votes, compared to Miss Jinnah's **36 %.**
- Results were challenged by the opposition who claimed that the voting had been rigged.
- Riots began in Karachi and East Pakistan in which 20 people were killed.
- Ayub khan had been reelected.

A New capital:

- Since partition the capital had been Karachi.
- In 1959 the site of Islamabad was chosen to replace Karachi as the Capital of Pakistan.
- In **1967** Islamabad was officially made the capital.
- Work on the city's principal buildings, streets, and facilities continued and were completed
by the mid-1970s.
- It is a modern and carefully planned city.
- The city is divided into 8 largely self-contained zones.

Agricultural reforms / the Green Revolution:

- An experiment of small subsistence holdings had never been efficient.
- A law was passed saying that no farm could be smaller than **12.5** acres or larger than **500** acres (irrigated) or **1000** acres (unirrigated).
- This meant that many smaller farmers found their land was redistributed.
- However the resulting larger farms did produce a steady rise in food output.
- Big landlords were forced to find tenants for parts of their land and this too raised productivity as the tenants and smaller farms were often more efficient than the larger , poorly run farms.
- Four dams were built to help irrigation.
- Loans were also given to farmers to build wells.
- Productivity was further increased due to mechanization.

Industrial reforms:

- Industrial development was also considered.
- This was carried out with the help of loans from more industrialized western countries.(USA, Germany, UK)
- In 1962 an *oil refinery* was established in Karachi and a Mineral development Corporation set up for the exploration of mineral deposits.

- In **1964** an Economic union was formed with Iran and Turkey, the Regional cooperation development (**RCD**) (to develop ties in Trade, Commerce and industry).
- An *Export Bonus Scheme* was set up offering incentives to industrialists who increased exports.
- The average annual rate by which the economy grew in the 1960 was **7 %**, three times that of India.
- But the new wealth created, did little to benefit the large numbers of Pakistanis living near the poverty line.
- It was revealed that just **22** families controlled 66 % of Pakistan's industrial assets.
- The same families also controlled 80 % of Pakistan's banking and insurance companies.
- A small elite group of wealthy Pakistanis had almost complete control of Pakistan's wealth.
- All these families belong to West Pakistan.
- Industry was improving rapidly but Pakistan was increasingly dependent on foreign aid.

Social and Educational reforms:

- New curriculum for schools and new textbooks were published.
- Government began an extensive literacy programme, building new schools and colleges.
- Ayub khan appointed **General Azam Khan** the *Rehabilitation Minister* to settle 75,000 refugees in newly built dwellings near Karachi.
- Laws were passed that factory owners had to provide accommodations for their workers at a reasonable rent.
- Family Planning Programmes were also launched (funded by America).
- Medical facilities were also improved.
- Medical and Nursing schools were also set up to increase the number of doctors and nurses.

Political unrest and downfall of Ayub:

- In **1965** Pakistan went to war with India over Kashmir.
- Neither side was able to win a decisive victory.
- Ayub told the people that Pakistan had won the war but the peace treaty at *Tashkent*

contained no reference to how the Kashmir issue should be settled.

- It was to regain that disputed Kashmir territory that Pakistan had started the war.
- Ayub sacked the foreign Minsiter, *Zulkiqar Ali Bhutto*, who he blamed for the failings in the war.
- Bhutto now became a focal point for opposition to Ayub.
- By 1968 many people were discontented with the government.
- It seemed to be undemocratic as there were numerous accusations of intimidation and vote rigging in the elections for the Electoral College and the presidential elections.
- The economy was improving yet only a few people were benefiting from this.
- Agricultural production was rising but so ere food prices.
- Ayub decided to celebrate the achievements of his ten years as head of state by declaring it

  "*A Decade of Development*", but this didn't end the growing opposition.
- In **October 1968**, there were student protests all over West Pakistan.
- On a visit to Peshawar Ayub was the target of a failed assassinations attempt.
- When Ayub carried out widespread arrests, including Bhutto, there were more protests, which spread to East Pakistan.
- Ayub Khan's repressive policies succeeded in uniting the various parries that opposed him.
- In **Jan. 1969** eight of them formed the Democratic Action Committee.
- They wanted proper election, the lifting of emergency powers and autonomy for East Pakistan.
- On **17 Feb. 1969** Ayub Khan withdrew the emergency powers and released

many political prisoners arrested in the previous Oct of 1968.

- He began negotiating with the opposition, but he had done too little too late.
- The opposition rapidly gained support whilst he and his party rapidly lost it.
- By March 1969 he realized that he didn't have enough support to stay in power.
- On **25 March 1969** he resigned.
- But he didn't call for new elections to choose another president.
- Instead he handed over power to the army and for the second time in its short history Pakistan experienced martial law.

Expected Questions:

<u>Question No.1:</u> Explain why the period of Ayub Khan.s government 1958-69 is called the Decade of Progress? (10)   June 99

Q.4 b

<u>Question No.2:</u> which of the following contributed the most to Pakistan's domestic policies:

Liaqat Ali Khan

Ayub Khan

Zia ul Haq

Explain your answer with reference to all three of the above. (14)   June 2001

Q.4c

<u>Question No.3:</u> Why was Martial Law declared in 1958? (7)   Nov.2002

Q.4 b <u>Question No.4:</u> Which of the following was the most important contribution of ayub Khan's government during the Decade of Development between 1958 and 1969.

Agricultural and econo,ic reforms

Constitutional reforms

Foreign policy?

Explain your answer with reference to all three above. (14)   Nov.2003

Q.4c

<u>Question No.5:</u> Why was Martial Law declared in 1958? (7)   Nov.2004

Q.4 b <u>Question No.6:</u> Constitutional Reforms were the most important of Ayub Khan's domestic policies during the decade of development between 1958 and 1969. Do you agree? Give reasons for your answer. (14)   June 2005

Q.5 c

Question No.7: Why did Ayub declare Martial Law in 1958? (7)   Nov.2006

Q.5 b **Question No.8:** Ayub Khan's agricultural reforms were more successful than any other of his domestic policies between 1958-1969. Do you agree or disagree? Give reasons for your answer. (14) Nov 2007 Q.4 c

Question No.9: Why were the years 1958-1969 called the decade of Progress? (7) June 2010 Q. 5 b

Question No, 10: What was the Basic Democratic System of Ayub Khan? (4)   Nov 2011Q.4 a

Question No.11: Constitutional reforms were the most important of Ayub Khan's domestic policies during the 'Decade of Progress' between 1958 and 1969.' Do you agree? Give reasons for your answer.(14)   June 2012

Q. 5 c

Question No. 12: why was Martial Law declared by Ayub Khan in 1958? (4) Nov.2012 Q.4 b

Question No. 13: Were the social reforms of Ayub Khan the most important of his domestic policies
during the 'Decade of Progress' between 1958 and 1969? Explain your answer. (14)June 2014 Q.4 c

 Question No. 14: In 1962, Ayub Khan introduced a new constitution that was largely made up of his own proposals. The new constitution was aimed at making Ayub Khan's position more secure and guaranteed far-reaching powers for the President. It was disliked by many people, especially those in East Pakistan who felt that they would have little part in governing Pakistan. As a result within a decade there was a need to introduce a new constitution.

(a) Describe the terms of the 1973 Constitution. [4]   Nov.2014 Q.4 a

Topic 27
GENERAL YAHYA KHAN and the creation of Bangladesh 1971
Introduction

The **_Tashkent Declaration_** signed by the Indian Prime Minister **_Lal Bahadur Shastri_** and the Pakistani **_President Muhammad Ayub Khan_** was not at all approved by the general public, and was regarded as submission to India and humiliation for the nation. Politicians were already unhappy with Ayub Khan whose Government was celebrating the decade of various reforms. But he fell victim to the then Foreign Minister, **_Zulfiqar Ali Bhutto,_** who exploited the whole situation. He resigned from office and after forming a party of his own, Pakistan Peoples Party, announced to "_defeat the great dictator with the power of the people_". As a result, he and others were arrested.

Ayub Khan tried his best to handle the situation by releasing a number of political prisoners, including the most popular leader of East Pakistan, Sheikh Mujib-ur-Rahman. He held a Round Table Conference in Rawalpindi with all the well-known political leaders in March 1969, but it proved to be a stalemate, with the result that Ayub Khan was forced to hand over power to General Muhammad Yahya Khan, on **_March 25, 1969._** Pakistan was now under the grip of another Martial Law.

Being deeply aware of the explosive political situation in the country, General Yahya Khan decided to transfer power to the elected representatives of the people and announced that the general elections would be held on October 5, 1970.

KEY POINTS:

- Following the declaration of martial law, the C-In-C of the army, General Yahiya khan was appointed Chief Martial law administrator and also took over as President.
- He announced that

1. _Basic democracy_ had not been a success.
2. There would be a properly elected government.
3. The **_one unit system_** had not worked, so there would be a return to Provincial government.
- Yahiya was committed to bringing democracy to Pakistan based on "_one man one vote_".
- The one unit plan and the 1962 Constitution were annulled and Pakistan's four provinces re-established.
- From **Jan 1970** political activity resumed.
- The various parties began campaigning to elect a National assembly of 300 members.
- The assembly would have 120 days to draw up a new constitution.
- The elections were to be held in OCT 1970 but they had to be postponed because severe flooding in East Pakistan caused such chaos that voting was impossible.
- The elections were finally held on **7 Dec. 1970** and for the first time ever were held on the principle of one man one vote.
- The results were such a shock that they created constitutional crises in Pakistan.

Results:

- The election gave _Pakistan Peoples Party (PPP)_ led by Zulfikar Ali Bhutto, 81 of the 138 seats in West Pakistan.

- There were 162 seats in East Pakistan and one party the popular *Awami League,* led by *Sheikh Mujib- ur-Rehman* won almost all of them.
- The Awami League had contested the election on a manifesto calling for political and economic independence for East Pakistan.
- The AL would also have a majority in the NA.
- Yahya could not allow the traditional dominance of West Pakistan to be overthrown.
- The AL won **160** of the **162** seats in East Pakistan because a sense of frustration felt by the people of in East Pakistan towards their countrymen in West Pakistan.
- West Pakistani felt their culture to be superior than east Pakistanis.
- Ruling class of West Pakistan believed that East Pakistan was not well represented in any aspect of Pakistan's administration, not for judiciary, not for civil service.
- In the army too the majority of f officers were from West Pakistan.
- These resentments caused the people of East Pakistan to vote in overwhelming numbers for a party which promised them a real say in how Pakistan was governed.
- There were no botheration of economic development in East Pakistan.
- West Pakistanis were 15 % wealthier than east Pakistanis.
- There was the transferring of resources from east to West Pakistan.
- The single largest Pakistani export was jute which was grown in East Pakistan.
- The largest spending was on defense to protect the western Pakistani border with India.(no dispute between Eastern Pakistan and India).
- More than that the AL won their huge victory by campaigning on the basis of the <u>six</u> points.

(i)   A directly elected government.

(ii)   The federal government to control defense and foreign policy .all other decisions to be made at provincial level.

(iii)   Separate currencies and financial policies foe East Pakistan, to stop all the money flowing from East Pakistan to West Pakistan.

(iv)   The provinces to tax their people and send a share to the federal government. The federal government not to tax people.

(v)   Each province to set up its own trade agreements with other countries and to control the money spent through this trade.

(vi)   Each province to have its own troops.

West Pakistan reacts:

- In Jan 1971, Yahya visited Mujib-ur-rehman to persuade him not to form the next government and that he should not use the new assembly to create a new constitution limiting the power of the central government.
- In Feb 1971, Bhutto announced that the PPP would not join National Assembly unless Mujib reached an agreement about power sharing.
- On 1st March 1971, Yahya postponed the opening of the assembly without setting a new date.

- The people of East Pakistan considered that they had been betrayed and immediately began a campaign of civil disobedience, strikes, demonstrations and refusing to pay taxes.
- When it became clear that the power of the central government had broken down in East Pakistan yahya appointed **General Tikka Khan** as Chief Martial law administrator there.
- On 15 March Yahiya and Bhutto met Mujib in Dhaka for talks to resolve the situation but no agreement could be reached.
- On 25 March yahya flew back to Islamabad and the next day Bhutto also left Dhaka.
- That night Tikka's men moved in on the AL, Mujib was arrested and hundreds of his supporters and colleagues were arrested or killed.

The outbreak of Civil War:

- Yahiya sent the army into East Pakistan to Keep Order and the AL was banned.
- Yahiya claimed that Mujib was claiming to declare independence.
- On 26 March the Sovereign Republic of Bangladesh was announced in a secret radio broadcast from Dhaka.
- The government reaction was harsh, thousands of Bengali's were killed, press censorship was imposed and all political activity throughout Pakistan was control of East Pakistan.
- Yahiya ordered the Pakistan army to take control of East Pakistan.
- The measures were supported by all the political parties in West Pakistan and Bhutto claimed tat *"Pakistan has been saved"*.
- Rather then being saved the reality was millions of Bengali refugees were across the border to India and civil war was now inevitable.
- On 31 March India declared its supporter for "the people of Bengal" against west Pakistan and train a rebel Bengali army called *Mukti Bhani*.
- Yahiya Khan sent more troops into East Pakistan and by early April the army had gained control of most of the major towns and was successful in driving off the east Pakistani rebels.
- On 21 Nov. the Mukti Bhani launched an attack on Jessore knowing that the Indians were supporting the rebel forces.

War with India:

- On 3rd December Pakistani air force launched attack on northern India to prevent East Pakistan.
- On 4rth December India attacked East Pakistan from air, ground and sea simultaneously.
- With in two weeks the Indian forces had surrounded Dhaka.
- The Pakistan Army tried to divert the Indian army from East Pakistan by launching attacks in Kashmir and Punjab.
- The UN Security Council had been trying to find a solution to avoid war.

- Bhutto attended UN talks in NY and a resolution was passed calling on India and Pakistan to stop fighting and withdraw from East Pakistan.
- No proper solution was carried out due to veto of Russia in favor of India.
- Bhutto returned to Pakistan knowing that Pakistan had to win the war on its own.
- Just a week after arrived in Pakistan, Yahiya accepted defeat and ordered the army in East Pakistan to surrender.
- The separation of East Pakistan came as huge shock to the people of West Pakistan.

Reason for defeat:

- The main reason for the army's failure was that the people of East Pakistan were determined to resist West Pakistan.
- Muslim soldiers had little heart for such a fight in which they would have to put up armed resistance against fellow Muslims.
- There wasn't any support of allies for Pakistan particularly from China and USA.
- India was properly supported by USSR and by the Bengalis themselves.
- Weak and indecisive role of UNO.

Consequences of war:

- Defeat brought disgrace for yayha and for the army.
- On **20 December 1971** Yahya resigned as President and replaced by Bhutto.
- On **21 December 1971**, the Republic of Bangladesh was officially declared.
- In Jan 1972 Bhutto released Mujib from prison.
- On 10 Jan 1972 Mujib became the first Prime Minister of Bangladesh.

Reasons for Separation of East Pakistan 1971:

East Pakistan was at a distance of 1600 km from the west wing with a large hostile Indian territory in between. Had East Pakistan been contiguous to west Pakistan, the separation would never have taken place. Political grievances of the people of east Pakistan was one of the most important reasons .the province had a larger population (56%) but their political power was in the hands of west wing politicians. They had the grievances of underrepresentation. They demanded more seats in the central assembly and the greater share in the cabinets because of the larger population.

They were always more ministers from the west wing than from east Wing in all cabinets. The long presidential rule of ayub khan increased their sense of deprivation. After the election of 1970 when Awami League won majority of seats in the national assembly Mujib was not allowed to become the PM of Pakistan and to from his cabinet.

The other important reason was economic. The export of raw jute from EP was the main source of foreign exchange earnings and revenue to central government. This earning was spent more on the development of the west wing. And the east wing received a small share of development funds.

Greater and faster industrial development took place in west wing. The industrial units opened in EP mostly belonged to the industrialist of West Pakistan. The result was that there was the continual transfer of capital from east wing to west wing. Most of the banks insurance companies and big commercial firms had their head offices at Karachi. There was greater prosperity in west wing and more poverty in east wing.

The behaviors of west pak. Administrative officers who were posted in East Pakistan were hateful and humiliating with the Bengalis. Hatred developed between the people of east Pakistani people and west Pakistani people. India's hostile propaganda also poisoned the minds of the people of EP.
In the armed forces Bengalis share was only 10 percent. People of EP felt deprived .East Pakistan's share in central government services was only 15 percent
The language problem was also an important reason. It was a big hurdle in creating solidarity and unity in the Pakistani nation.

Indian military intervention became the immediate reason. Indian army attacked and entered in EP from many sides in Nov. 1971. This resulted in surrendered of Pakistani army in 16 Dec 1971 when Bangladesh created.

SHEIKH MUJIB:
Sheikh Mujib-ur-Rahman was born on March 22, 1922, at Faridpur, now in Bangladesh. He was an active member of the Muslim League in pre-Independence India. After Independence, Mujib-ur-Rahman remained active in politics. As a law student in March 1948, he was arrested for leading a black-flag demonstration against Jinnah on the issue of making Urdu as the State language. Along with **H. S. Suhrawardy**, he organized the Awami League in 1949.

After the death of Suhrawardy, Mujib-ur-Rahman revived the *Awami League* as a political party in January 1965. This time to contest the presidential elections as a component of the **Combined Opposition Party**, which nominated Miss Fatima Jinnah as the opposition candidate for the presidential post against the candidature of Ayub Khan.

The newborn country's initial Government was formed in January 1972, under the leadership of Sheikh Mujib-ur-Rahman, who became the Prime Minister. In early 1975, Mujib-ur-Rahman became the President. He was, however, unable to stabilize the political situation, and was assassinated in a military coup on August 15, 1975, at his residence. Khandaker Mushtaq Ahmad was made the new President of Bangladesh.

EXPECTED QUESTIONS:

Question No.1: Explain three reasons why Bangladesh was created in 1971. (7)   June 2000
Q.5 b **Question No.2:** Why did Mujib ur rehman and Awami League demand six points? (7)   June 2001
Q.5 b **Question No.3:** Why was Pakistan unsuccessful in the 1965 and 1971 wars against India? (7) June 2002 Q.5 b
Question No.4: Why did East Pakistan wish to break away from Pakistan? (7)   June 2003 Q.4 b
Question No. 5: Why was India successful in the 1965 and 1971 wars against Pakistan? (7) June 2006 Q.4 b
Question No.6: The six points made by Mujib ur Rehman and the Awami League was the most important factor in the creation of Bangladesh in 1971. Do you agree? Give reasons for your answer.(14) June 2006 Q.4 c **Question No. 7:** the geographical position of East Pakistan was the most important reason for the creation of Bangladesh in 1981. Do you agree or disagree? Give reasons for your answer. (14)   Nov 2007 Q.
5 c **Question No.8:** Were economic factors more important than any other factor in the creation of Bangladesh in 1971? Explain your answer. (14)   June 2009 Q.5c
Question No.9: political factors were more important than any other factor in the creation of Bangladesh in 1971. Do you agree or disagree? Give reasons for your answer. (14)   June 2011 Q.
5 c **Question No. 10:** why was India successful in the 1965 and 1971 wars against Pakistan? (7) June 2012 Q.5 b

Topic 28

ZULFIKAR ALI BHUTTO

Introduction

Zulfiqar Ali Bhutto was born on **January 5, 1928.** He was the only son of **Sir Shah Nawaz Bhutto**. Zulfiqar Ali Bhutto married **Nusrat Isphahani** on September 8, 1951 and in 1953, his first child, Benazir Bhutto, was born on June 21.

In 1958, he joined President Iskander Mirza's Cabinet as Commerce Minister. He was the youngest Minister in Ayub Khans Cabinet. In 1963, he took over the post of Foreign Minister from Muhammad Ali Bogra. In June 1966, Bhutto left Ayub's Cabinet over differences concerning the **Tashkent Agreement.**

Zulfiqar Ali Bhutto launched **Pakistan Peoples Party** after leaving Ayub's Cabinet. In the general elections held in December 1970, P. P. P. won a large majority in West Pakistan but failed to reach an agreement with **Sheikh Mujib-ur-Rahman**, the majority winner from East Pakistan. Following the 1971 War and the separation of East Pakistan, Yahya Khan resigned and Bhutto took over as President and **Chief Martial Law Administrator on December 20, 1971.**

Following a political crisis in the country, Bhutto was imprisoned by General Zia-ul-Haq, who imposed **Martial Law on July 5, 1977.**

On April 4, 1979, the former Prime Minister was hanged, after the Supreme Court upheld the death sentence passed by the Lahore High Court. The High Court had given him the death sentence on charges of murder of Mohammad ali raza khan kasuri.

Zulfiqar Ali Bhutto was buried in his ancestral village at **Garhi Khuda Baksh**, next to his father's grave.

KEY POINTS:

Political reforms:

- *20 December 1971*, Zulfikar ali Bhutto became President and chief martial law administrator.
- The 1970 election however had given the PPP an overwhelming majority in the NA.
- He was determined to **limit the powers of the army** so that it would not intervene to thwart his policies.
- He removed the most important army leaders (29 in Bhutto's first four months in power).amongst these were the head of the Air Force, Air Marshal Rahim khan and the C.in-C of the army, General Gul Hasan.
- Appointing his own leaders for example, *General Tikka Khan* was placed in charge of the army in a new post named "Chief of Army Staff".
- Setting up the **FSF** from October 1972, a government controlled military force set up "assist the police force".

The Simla Agreement:

- On **2 July 1972** Bhutto signed the Simla agreement with the Prime minister of India, *Indira Gandhi*.
- India agreed to return prisoners of war to Pakistan in return for a promise from Pakistan that the Kashmir problem would be discussed directly with India and not in international forums such as UN.
- Bhutto's popularity increased by bringing home the prisoners of war.

Establishing a new constitution:

- In April 1972 martial law was lifted and a new assembly was called.
- A committee was set up with representatives from different parties in the assembly to draw up a new constitution.
- The committee reported in April 1973 and its recommendations received almost unanimous support in the Assembly.
- On **14 august 1973** the new constitution became law.
- The most significant features of the new constitution were:

(i)   There would be two houses, the senate and the Assembly. The assembly would be elected for a period of 5 years and the members of the senate would be nominated in equal numbers from each of the 4 provinces.

(ii)   The leader of the party with a majority in the Assembly would become PM and select a cabinet.

(iii)   The president became largely a figurehead, whose orders had to be signed by the PM.

(iv)   Pakistan was an Islamic Republic and both the PM and president had to be Muslims.

(v)   Pakistan was a federal state. Each province had its own assembly, elected by universal adult suffrage with the majority party forming the provincial government. The national Assembly could only change the political leadership in the provinces by amending the constitution which required at least a 75 % majority in a vote.

(vi)   All fundamental basic human rights were guaranteed.

- As a leader of the PPP, Bhutto became PM and Chaudhri Fazal Elahi elected President.

Industrial Reforms:

- Bhutto wanted to bring down inflation from 25 %.
- For that he introduced the programme of **nationalization.**
- The sugar, cotton, vegetable oil and rice industries together with the banking and insurance sectors were taken under the government control.
- 70 major industrial units were placed under the control of a Federal Ministry of production.
- These changes were designed to help the government in the following ways:

(i)   Control industrial output and channel investment into industrialization.

(ii)   Raise the workers living and working standards including the provision of cheap housing.

(iii)   Allow the workers to set up unions.

(iv)   To erase the inequalities that had collected most of the industrial wealth into a few hands. 20 industrial houses owned 80 % of Pakistan's large scale industry.

(v)   Create wealth to help fund other government reforms.

(vi)   Raise the popularity of the PPP.

Problems for nationalization policy:

(i) Pakistan's education system was not yet producing sufficiently educated workers to take managerial positions in the industries under the Federal Ministry of Production.

(ii) Capable factory owner were often replaced by civil servants with little understanding of commerce.

(iii) The changes took place at a time when the world was going through a recession .the nationalized industries faced a declining demand for their goods across the world and private companies were forced to close.

- Despite these problems Bhutto's industrial reforms did have some success and inflation fell to just **6 %** in 1976.
- Economic growth also began to increase.

Agricultural reforms:

- Bhutto believed that improved technology and better farming methods had raised production.
- So landowners could maintain their income on smaller, more productive, areas of land.
- He therefore *cut the ceiling to 250 acres from 500 acres irrigated and 500 from 1000 acres un-irrigated.*
- The surplus land could be sold to the smaller peasant/farmers to make better profits.
- The cunning big landlords started transferring their holding to their members or to their trusted tenants.
- Bribery and corruption emerged among patwaris.

- Bhutto also wanted to give tenants security of tenure of the land they farmed.
- The tenants can purchase their farmed land from landlord but cannot sell to a third party who might then evict the tenants.
- Such a measure encouraged tenants to make improvements on their lands as they knew they knew they would not be evicted.

Education:

- The standard of education was very deplorable.
- Only 50 % children attending the school and literary rate were 25 %.
- Bhutto's government outlined 8 ambitious goals.

(i) to eradicate ignorance
(ii) Education for all including women, mentally impaired and illiterate adults.
(iii) To ensure that the curriculum meets Pakistan's social, economic and political needs.
(iv) To ensure uniformity of education
(v) To raise the self confidence of the common man.
(vi) To raise aspiration for higher education.
(vii) To develop each person's personality and potential.
(viii) To develop Pakistani culture and identity.

- Government nationalized all private schools and colleges to remove discrepancies.
- More schools were built to provide free primary education for all.

Problems for new education policies:

- In remote areas these policies were not implemented effectively.
- Only 13 % budget was allocated for education which was not sufficient.
- Education was free even then rural people couldn't afford the loss of earnings they faced it they sent a child to school instead of sending it out to work.
- Standard of education was not maintained due to high strength of students.
- Non availability of trained teachers.
- Instead of all the government efforts the literacy rate was not increased more than 1 %.

Health and Social Reforms:

- Pakistan had the highest infant mortality rate and life expectancy was very low.
- In august 1972 Bhutto launched a health scheme designed to correct these anomalies.

(i) He introduced Rural Health Centre (RHCs) and Basic Health Units (BHUs) in urban areas to provide more widespread healthcare. The plan was to set up 1 RHC for every 60,000 people and 1 BHU for every 20,000 people.

(ii) Training colleges for doctors and nurses were expected to admit students on merits. Once qualified, doctors had to work the first year wherever the government placed them.

(iii) The sale of medicines under brand names was also banned which reduced the costs of medicines. Medicines were made available without prescription.

Problems for health policies:

- There were always a shortage of doctors and nurses.
- The removal of brand names from medicines also saw a fall in the income of chemists and many international drug companies closed down their operations in Pakistan as they could not make profits.

The 1977 elections:

- Bhutto called a general election in 1977 and confident of victory.
- Once the election was called 9 of the various opposition parties combined to form the **Pakistan National Alliance (PNA).**
- They all wanted to end rule of Bhutto (PPP) and to enforce Islamic Law in Pakistan.
- PNA started gaining support but their rallies were attacked by the Bhutto's supporters.
- The government introduced a law limiting public gatherings to just 5 people to stop public support for PNA.
- The results of the elections showed a landslide victory for the PPP.
- Of the 200 seats contested PPP won 154 against the PNA's 38.
- PNA accused the government of rigging and demanded new elections.

Steps to downfall:

- Bhutto refused to agree to refresh elections and PNA organized mass protests against the government.
- He offered fresh elections in some of the disputed constituencies and to appease the religious factions, banned gambling, restricted the sale of alcohol, declared Friday to be the weekly holiday.

- On 19 April he declared a state of emergency placing Pakistan under Martial Law.

- PNA leadership was arrested and 10,000 supporters were in prison.
- Consequently on 5 July the army staged a coup, named: "*Operation Fairplay*".
- Bhutto and all other political leaders were arrested that night.
- Two days later the chief of army staff General Muhammad Zia-ul-Haq announced the suspending of the constitution and the dissolution of all national and provincial assemblies.
- Once more the army was in control in Pakistan.

EXPECTED QUESTIONS:

Question No.1: how successful was ZAB as P.M of Pakistan. Explain your answer. (14)

June 2000 Q.4 c

Question No.2: give the reasons why ZAB was executed in 1979. (7)   NOV. 2000 Q.5 b

Question No.3: in which of the following did ZAB have most success, Reform and control of the armed forces
Constitutional reform Education and
health reforms?
Explain your answer with reference to all three of the above. (14)   NOV 2002 Q.4 c

Question no 4: why did ZAB fall from power in 1979? (7)   June 2003 Q.5 b

Question No.5: Constitutional reforms were the most important of ZAB's domestic policies between 1971 and 1977.do you agree? Give reasons for your answer. (14)   June 2004 Q.5 c

Question No. 6: social reforms were the most important of ZAB's domestic policies between 1971 and 1977. Do you agree? Give reasons for your answer. (14)   June 2006 Q.5 c

Question No. 7: why was ZAB arrested and subsequently executed in 1979? (7)   NOV 2007 Q.5 b.

Question No.8: education reforms were the most important of ZAB's domestic policies between 1971 and1977. Do you agree? Give reasons for your answer. (14)   NOV 2008 Q. 4 c

Question No.9: Why did ZAB come to power in 1971? (7)   NOV 2009 Q.5 b

Question No.10: what was the Simla Agreement? (4)   NOV 2010 Q.5 a

Question No. 11: In December 1971, Zulfikar Ali Bhutto became President and Chief Martial Law Administrator. His party had an overwhelming majority in the National Assembly and he was determined to introduce radical measures to bring about changes in Pakistan. He established a constitution and introduced a range of domestic measures relating to industry, agriculture, education and administrative, health and social reforms. However, he was unable to stay in power and fell from office before the end of the decade.

Describe Bhutto's downfall from power. (4)   Nov. 2012 Q. 5a

General Zia ul Haq 1977-1988

Introduction

General Muhammad Zia-ul-Haq was the one who enforced Martial Law for the third time in the brief history of Pakistan. Second child and eldest son of **Muhammad Akram,** a teacher in the British Army, Zia-ul-Haq was born on **August 12, 1924, at Jalandhar.**

He was commissioned in the British Army in 1943 and served in Burma, Malaya and Indonesia during World War II. On **April 1, 1976, in a surprise move the then Prime Minister of Pakistan, Zulfiqar Ali Bhutto, appointed Zia-ul-Haq as Chief of Army Staff,** superseding five senior Generals. Bhutto probably wanted somebody as the head of the armed forces who would not prove to be a threat for him, and the best available option was the simple General who was apparently interested only in offering prayers and playing golf. However, history proved that General Zia-ul- Haq proved to be much smarter than Bhutto thought. When political tension reached its climax due to the deadlock between Bhutto and the leadership of **Pakistan National Alliance** on the issue of general elections, Zia-ul-Haq took advantage of the situation. On July 5, 1977, he carried out a bloodless coup overthrowing Bhutto's government and enforced Martial Law in the country.

After assuming power as Chief Martial Law Administrator, Zia-ul-Haq *promised to hold National and Provincial Assembly elections in the next 90 days* and to hand over power to the representatives of the Nation. However, in October 1977, he announced the postponement of the electoral plan and decided to start an *accountability process* of the politicians. In a statement, he said that he changed his decision due to the strong public demand for the scrutiny of political leaders who had indulged in malpractice in the past. The Disqualification Tribunal was formulated and many former Members of Parliament were disqualified from participating in politics at any level for the next seven years. PPP was also banned.

In the mid-1980s, Zia-ul-Haq decided to fulfill his promise of holding elections in the country. But before handing over the power to the public representatives, he decided to secure his position. *Referendum was held in the county in December 1984,* and the masses were given the option to elect or reject the General as the future President of Pakistan. **The question asked in the referendum was phrased in a way that Zia-ul-Haq's victory was related to the process of Islamization in the country.** According to the official result, more than 95 percent of the votes were cast in favour of Zia-ul-Haq, thus he was elected as President for the next five years.

After being elected President, Zia-ul-Haq decided to hold *elections in the country in February 1985 on a non-party basis*. Most of the political parties decided to boycott the elections but election results showed that many victors belonged to one party or the other. To make things easier for himself, the General nominated the Prime Minister from amongst the Members of the Assembly. To many, his nomination of *Muhammad Khan Junejo* as the Prime Minister was because he wanted a simple person at the post who would act as a puppet in his hands. Before handing over the power to the new Government he made certain **Amendments in the Constitution** and got them endorsed from the Parliament before lifting the state of emergency in the county. Due to this *Eighth Amendment* in the Constitution, the powers of the President were increased to an absolute level.

On *May 29, 1988, Zia-ul-Haq dissolved the National Assembly and removed the Prime Minister under article 58(2)* **b** of the amended Constitution.

After 11 years, Zia-ul-Haq once again made the same promise to the Nation to hold fresh elections within next 90 days. With **Benazir Bhutto** back in the country and the Muslim League leadership annoyed with the President over the decision of May 29, Zia-ul-Haq was trapped in the most difficult situation of his political life. The only option left for him was to repeat history and to postpone the elections once again.

However, before taking any decision, *Zia-ul-Haq died in an air crash near Bhawalpur on August 17, 1988.* The accident proved to be very costly for the country as almost the entire military elite of Pakistan was on board. Though United States' Ambassador to Pakistan was also killed in the misfortune, the remains of Zia-ul-Haq were buried in the premises of Faisal Mosque, Islamabad. His death brought a large number of mourners to attend his funeral, including a large number of Afghanis.

During his rule, Zia-ul-Haq tried his utmost to maintain close ties with the Muslim World. He made vigorous efforts along with other Muslim States to bring an end to the war between Iran and Iraq. Pakistan joined the Non-Aligned Movement in 1979 during Zia-ul-Haq's term. He also fought a war by proxy in Afghanistan and saved Pakistan from a direct war with Soviet Union.

Islamisation under ZIA:

In his first address to the nation, he declared that Islamic laws would be enforced and his attention would be devoted towards establishing the Islamic society for which Pakistan had been created. General Zia wanted to bring the legal, social, economic and political institutions of the country in conformity with the Islamic principles, values and traditions in the light of Quran and Sunnah, to enable the people of Pakistan to lead their lives in accordance to Islam.

The Government of Zia-ul-Haq took a number of steps to eradicate non-Islamic practices from the country. He introduced the *Zakat, Ushr, Islamic Hadood and Penal Code* in the country. The Government invited eminent scholars to compile laws about Islamic financing. The Zakat and Ushr Ordinance to Islamize the economic system was promulgated on June 20, 1980. **Zakat** was to be deducted from bank accounts of Muslims at the rate of 2.5 percent annually above the balance of Rupees 3,000. **Ushr** was levied on the yield of agricultural land in cash or kind at the rate of 10 percent of the agricultural yield, annually.

The Government appointed Central, Provincial, District and Tehsil Zakat Committees to distribute Zakat funds to the needy, poor, orphans and widows. **Shias** were exempted from Zakat deduction from their accounts due to their own religious beliefs. The Zakat was to be deducted by banks on the first day of Ramazan.

A **Federal Shariah** Court was established to decide cases according to the teachings of the Holy Quran and Sunnah. Appeals against the Lower and High Courts were to be presented before the Shariah Court for hearing. Blasphemy of the Holy Prophet (S. A. W.) would now be punishable by death instead of life imprisonment.

Zia-ul-Haq selected his **Majlis-i-Shoora in 1980**. It was to be the Islamic Parliament and act as the Parliament of Pakistan in place of the National Assembly. Most of the members of the Shoora were intellectuals, scholars, ulema, journalists, economists and professionals belonging to different fields of life. The Shoora was to act as a board of advisors for the President.

A number of other Islamization programs were carried out including the teaching of **Islamic Studies and Arabic**, which were made compulsory. **Pakistan Studies** and **Islamic Studies** were made compulsorily for B. A., B. Sc., Engineering, M. B. B. S., Commerce, Law and Nursing students. For professional studies, extra marks were given to people who were Hafiz-e-Quran.

A **Shariah Council** consisting of ulema was established to look into the constitutional and legal matters of the State in order to bring them in line with Islamic thought. Since Islam does not allow interest, On January 1, 1980, Muhammad Zia-ul-Haq introduced a **"Profit and Loss Sharing System"** according to which an account holder was to share the loss and profit of the bank. The media was also targeted. Television especially was brought under the Islamization campaign, **news in Arabic** were to be read on both television and radio, female anchor persons were required to cover their heads, the **Azan** was relayed regularly on radio and television to announce time for prayers.

In the armed forces, the status of the religious teachers was raised to that of a Commissioned Officer. This was done to attract highly qualified individuals from the universities and religious institution to serve on such assignments.

As the government grew further in its Islamic leanings, the numbers of mosques were increased. *Ordinance for the sanctity of Ramazan* was introduced to pay reverence to the holy month of Ramazan. The Ordinance forbade public drinking and eating during the holy month of Ramazan. A three months imprisonment and a fine of Rupees 500 were imposed for violating the Ordinance. A program to ensure the regularity of prayers called the Nizam-i-Salaat was launched by General Zia himself.

Zia's Government introduced the **Hadood Ordinance** for the first time in Pakistan, which meant the punishments *ordained by the Holy Quran or Sunnah on the use of liquor, theft, adultery and qazf.* Under this Ordinance, a culprit could be sentenced to lashing, life imprisonment and in some cases, death by stoning.

General Zia-ul-Haq wanted to make Pakistan the citadel of Islam so that it could play an honorable and prominent role for the Islamicworld.

ECONOMIC REFORMS:

In **economic** affairs Zia announced the policy of **denationalization** of industries. Some nationalized industries were returned to the owner. Incentives were given in the form of fiscal and monetary concessions, and in import of machinery and raw material. Foreign investment was welcomed and full protection was granted. Industrialization gradually started and Zia's policy was successful. **Steel mill** was completed and **Karakorum highway** was built. Industrial and agricultural production showed an increase. Therefore it can be said that Zia had most success in economic affairs.

POLITICAL REFORMS:

Pakistan got the membership of NAM in 1979. Zia attended Havana conference and clarified Pakistan's nuclear policy and other issues. Zia attended the **OIC** meetings and gave full support to the Arab cause in Palestine. Zia supported the **afghan mujahidin** against the Russian forces in Afghanistan. With American military and financial help Russian forces were pushed out in 1988. Zia's Afghanistan policy and foreign policy was a success.

Zia promised election within 90 days. But he established a nominated Assembly called Majlis-e – shoora which had limited powers and worked from 1981 to 1985. In 1985 elections were held on non-party basis and re-elected assembly was formed. **M. khan junejo** became the PM and martial law was lifted. But Junejo govt. was dismissed and assembly was dissolved in May 1988. Zia promised fresh elections in Oct. 1988.

Afghan War Settlement:

In 1979, Russian forces invaded Afghanistan. Communism came to the threshold of Pakistan when forces led by Babrak Karmel overthrew the Government of Afghanistan. Some 120,000 Russian troops entered Afghanistan .The Afghan people organized a resistance force against this blatant aggression. The Soviet forces suffered greatly in terms of manpower and material, and the Afghan War proved expensive even for a world power like the Soviet Union.

General Zia stood against the spread of communism. The arms provided to Afghanistan freedom fighters were also provided to the Pakistan Army. As a result the Pakistan Army became better equipped.

Ultimately Negotiations on Afghanistan were carried out under Zia's Government, and the **Geneva** Accord was signed on April 14, 1988, under which the Soviet Union agreed to withdraw its forces in two instalments .The Soviet Government lived up to its commitment of withdrawal of forces according to the agreed timetable.

The victory in Afghanistan was achieved at a great cost to Pakistan. It had to look after and feed more than three million Afghan refugees that had crossed over to Pakistan. The refugees were a great economic burden on Pakistan. Not only this but, they also caused the problem of drugs and gunrunning in the country.

Mohammad Khan Junejo becomes PM 1985 to 1988:

After the Presidential referendum of December 1984, elections for the National and Provincial Assemblies were held in February 1985 on a non-party basis. President Zia-ul-Haq nominated Muhammad Khan Junejo as the Prime Minister of Pakistan on March 20, 1985.

After the lifting of Martial Law, Junejo tried to take a course independent of Zia. He annoyed military generals by withdrawing big staff cars from them and replacing them with small cars. He tried to conduct an independent foreign policy, particularly on Afghanistan, by taking into confidence and consulting leaders of political parties, including Benazir Bhutto, the leader of the Pakistan People's Party. His government even tried to probe into the military fiasco at the *Ojheri Camp near Islamabad on April 10, 1988,* which resulted in the death and serious injuries to a large number of civilians. This probe perhaps became the immediate cause for the dismissal of his government.

General Zia dismissed Junejo's Government using the controversial rule under **Article 58(2)** b of the Constitution Fresh elections were promised after 90 days but were eventually held on November 16, 1988, three months after Zia's death in a plane crash.

EXPECTED QUESTIONS:

Question no.1: was the promotion of Islamic values the most important achievement of General Zia between 1977-88? Explain your answer. (14)   Nov 2000 Q.5 c

Question No.2: which of the following contributed the most to Pakistan's domestic policies?

- Liaqat
  Ali Khan
  Ayub
  Khan
- Zia ul Haq

Explain your answer with reference to all three of the above. (14)   June 2001 Q.4c

Question No.3: how successful have governments been in the Islamization of Pakistan between 1947 and 1988? Explain your answer. (14)   June 2002 Q.5 c

Question No. 4: In which of the following did Zia have most success between 1977 and 1988:

Islamization Economic affairs   Political affairs

Explain your answer with reference to all three of the above. (14)   June 2003 Q.4 c

Question No.5: Islamic reforms were the most important of Zia ul Haq's domestic policies between 1977 and

1988. Do you agree? Give reasons for your answer. (14)   Nov 2005

Q.5 c Question No. 6: why did Zia introduce his Islamic reforms between 1977 and 1988? (7) June 2006 Q. 5 b

Question No. 7: Zia's foreign policy was more successful than his domestic reforms. Do you agree or disagree? Give reasons for your answer. (14)   June 2007 Q. 5 c

QuestionNo.8: why did ZIA introduce a series of Islamic laws between 1979 and 1988? (7)

                                                                                  June 2008 Q 5 b

Question No. 9: how successful have governments been in Islamization of Pakistan between 1947 and

1988? Explain your answer. (14)   Nov. 2009 Q. 5 c

QuestionNo.10: Islamic reforms were the most important of Zia's domestic policies between 1977 and 1988. Do

you agree or disagree? Give reasons for your answer. (14)   June 2010 Q. 4

c Question No. 11: Why did ZIA introduce his package of Islamic laws between 1979 and 1988? (7) June 2011

Q.5 c

Question No. 12: Was the promotion of Islamic values the most important achievement of General Zia-ul-Haq's

domestic policies between 1977 and 1988? Explain your answer. [14] Nov.2014 Q.4 C

BENAZIR BHUTTO AND NAWAZ SHARIF 1988 TO 1999:

Introduction

Benazir Bhutto, the eldest child of *Zulfiqar Ali Bhutto*, was born on *June 21, 1953,* at Karachi.She wanted to join the Foreign Service but her father wanted her to contest the Assembly election. Benazir Bhutto also assisted her father as an advisor.
In July 1977, General Zia-ul-Haq imposed Martial Law. During the Martial Law, Benazir was allowed to proceed abroad on medical grounds.

She returned on April 10, 1986, one million people welcomed her at the Lahore airport. She attended rallies all over Pakistan and supported the Movement for Restoration of Democracy. On *December 18, 1987, Benazir married Asif Ali Zardari* in Karachi. She contested the elections, which were held by *Ghulam Ishaq Khan,* who had taken over as acting President after the death of General Zia in an air crash on August 17, 1988, at Bhawalpur.

PPP won and Benair Bhutto became the first women to serve as Prime Minister in an Islamic country. Minister Benazir Bhutto announced that the *ban on Student Unions and Trade Unions would be lifted. The P. P. P. Government hosted the fourth S. A. A. R. C. Summit Conference in December 1988. As a result of the Conference, Pakistan and India finalized three peace agreements.*

BB faced a lot of problems since beginning. PPP gained majority in Sindh but not in other provinces.so she had to form a coalition with MQM but she had to face fierce opposition by IJI led by Nawaz Sharif who controlled the provincial government of Punjab. Other political parties also opposed him and within 11 months the opposition parties organised Non Confidence Motion in the National Assembly.

BB also faced resistance from ISI; Army couldn't support Benazir's government. Religious community also condemn women rule in Pakistan. Benazir also lost public support as it was unable to deliver on its promised employment and economic development. Education and health schemes couldn't be launched. Besides that she faced accusations that there was a corruption within her government and her husband Asif ali Zardari was later arrested on charges of blackmail and was jailed for two years. Her government was also faced to deal with the country's growing drug abuse problem.

Critical situation created when Sindhis and Mahajirs confrontation became severe. Widespread riots in Karachi ended MQM alliance with PPP in august 1989.BB also had the clashes with President and a major area of disagreements was over appointments to positions in the military and judiciary.

Serious conceptual differences arose between the P. P. P. Government and the Establishment. Less than two years later, on August 6, 1990, her Government was accused of corruption and dismissed by the President, Ghulam Ishaq Khan, who exercised his power through the controversial Eighth Amendment of the Constitution.

Her publications include *"Daughter of the East" and "Foreign Policy Perspective"*.

Fresh elections were scheduled on *October 24, 1990.* President Ghulam Ishaq Khan appointed Ghulam Mustafa Jatoi as the caretaker Prime Minister.

Nawaz sharif becomes PM 1990:

Elections for the National and Provincial Assemblies were held on October 24 and 27, 1990. Mian Muhammad Nawaz Sharif, the ex-Chief Minister of Punjab, was elected as the Prime Minister on November 1, 1990.

During his tenure as the Prime Minister, Nawaz Sharif made efforts to strengthen the industrial sector with the help of the private sector. National reconstruction programmes were launched. He introduced a policy of privatization of the industries which had been nationalized under Zulfikar Ali Bhutto. Projects like Ghazi Brotha and the Gwadar miniport were initiated. Land was distributed among landless peasants in Sindh. A massive uplift of Murree and Kahuta was done during his term as Chief Minister of Punjab. Relations with the Central Asian Muslim republics were strengthened and E. C. O. was given a boost. He also opened industries such as shipping, electricity supply , airlines and telecommunication. He imported thousands of yellow cabs to overcome unemployment. Cheap loans were provided. He also started nuclear programme which completed in 1998.

In an attempt to end the Afghan crisis, the **"Islamabad Accord"** was reached between various Afghan factions. A No Air Attack accord was also signed with India in 1991.His most important contribution was economic progress. The stupendous *Motorway project* was initiated that was completed during his second tenure.

Nawaz Sharif's Government remained in power till April 18 1993, when President Ghulam Ishaq Khan dissolved the National Assembly, once again exercising his power through the Eighth Amendment.

Reasons for Downfall:

Nawaz Sharif policies were undermined by lack of capital for investment. US support (aid) was also reduced after the soviet-Afghan war.

Pakistan's nuclear policy was badly criticized by US and other European Nations .reduction in overseas aid, high government spending and a decrease in remittances from overseas workers in Middle East placed severe pressure on Pakistan's finances.

One of the major banks operating in Pakistan; the Bank of credit and commerce international (BCCI) was also collapsed in 1991. That was the world's 7th largest bank .Sharif also lost support because of cooperative society's scandal. These societies had granted billions of rupees in loans to Sharif's family business, the ittefaq group.

Karachi's condition became further deteriorated. Gun carrying became the part of culture. Kidnappings, bombings and murders became common. Refugees from afghan war also created problem and heroin addicts also enhanced.

Most importantly sharif came into open conflict with, particularly after the death of General Asif Nawaz Janjua in Jan. 1993.Nawa sharif wanted his own chief of the army staff where as president appointed General Abdul waheed Kakar. Nawaz sharif wanted to change the 8TH amendment but president didn't want to do so. Consequently president dismissed sharif's government on 19th April in 1993 alleged corruption and mismanagement.

Moin Qureshi as caretaker PM:

On May 26, 1993, the Supreme Court of Pakistan declared the Presidential Order of the Assemblies' dissolution as unconstitutional and ruled for restoring the Nawaz Government and the National Assembly. However, because of the serious differences between the President Ghulam Ishaq Khan and the Prime Minister Mian Muhammad Nawaz Sharif, both resigned from their offices on July 18, 1993, along with the dissolution of the Central and Provincial Assemblies.

Moin Qureshi, a top World Bank official, was appointed as the Caretaker Prime Minister and chairman senate wassem sajjad was appointed as the caretaker President. Moin Qureshi was totally unknown in Pakistan; it was, however, felt that as he was a political outsider, he would remain neutral.

The only blot on Moin Qureshi's tenure as Prime Minister was that, in his last days, he made a large number of promotions and other administrative decisions in favor of his relatives.

BB becomes PM1993:

Benazir Bhutto returned to power for the second time in 1993 after the resignation of both President Ghulam Ishaq Khan and Prime Minister Nawaz Sharif on July 18, 1993. The resignation led to the announcement of fresh elections for the National and Provincial Assemblies. The elections were held on October 6 and 9, 1993, respectively.

The elections were boycotted by the M. Q. M. No party emerged with an absolute majority in the elections. As a result the P. P. P. formed the new government with the help of alliances. Benazir Bhutto took oath as Prime Minister on October 19, 1993. The Presidential election was held on November 13. **Farooq Ahmad Khan Leghari,** the P. P. P. candidate, won by 274 to 168 votes against the then acting President Wasim Sajjad.

During her second tenure, Benazir again faced trouble from the opposition. In 1994, Nawaz Sharif led a **"train march" from Karachi to Peshawar**. This was followed by general strike on September 20. Two weeks later Nawaz Sharif called a "wheel jam" strike on October 11.

BB also had to face confrontation with her mother Nusrat Bhutto who preferred Murtaza Bhotto as a leader for PPP. Murtaza also opposed Zardari's involvement in PPP. Later on Mir **Murtaza Bhutto was assassinated** under mysterious circumstances in a police ambush on September 20, 1996. The high-profile killing of her brother in her tenure damaged her political career.

Things were not going well between the President and Benazir's Government. Differences soon appeared and the Government felt that there was interference in the political matters of the Government by the President. President Farooq Leghari dismissed Benazir Bhutto's Government on charges of corruption and mismanagement on November 5, 1996, under the Article 58(2) b of the Eighth Amendment.

The second tenure of Benazir Bhutto was, however, highlighted by the **visit of the U. S. first Lady Hillary Clinton and her daughter Chelsea in 1995.** Hillary's visit considerably changed the world's perceptions about Pakistan and highlighted Pakistan as a liberal, modern and forward-looking country. In April 1994, Benazir visited the U. S., and projected Pakistan's stance on the F-16 fighter planes withheld by the U. S. despite payments. Her visit resulted in the passing of the Brown Amendment by the U. S. Senate on September 21, 1995, easing restrictions on Pakistan. It also helped in attracting foreign investors. On the domestic front she continued facing problems with M. Q. M. In spite of all her political endeavors, a smooth relationship could not be established between the Government and M. Q. M.

Malik Meraj becomes caretaker PM 1996:

President Sardar Farooq Leghari, exercising his powers through the Eighth Amendment, dismissed Benazir Bhutto's Government in November 1996, on charges of corruption and extra-judicial killings. After Benazir, **Malik Meraj Khalid, Rector of the International Islamic University,** was appointed as caretaker Prime Minister. The next elections were scheduled to be held on February 3, 1997.

Malik Meraj Khalid held the office of Prime Minister from November 5, 1996, to February 17, 1997.

Nawaz Sharif as PM 1996:

As scheduled, elections were held on February 3, 1997. Pakistan Muslim League won with an overwhelming majority with absolutely light and slight opposition. The Muslim League was able to obtain a two-third majority in the National Assembly and Mian Nawaz Sharif was re-elected as Prime Minister. He obtained a vote of confidence from the National Assembly on February 18, 1997.

A number of very important Constitutional Amendments were introduced during Nawaz Sharif's second term. These include the termination of the Eighth Amendment, passing of the **Thirteenth Amendment** and the Ehtesab Act, 1997. Nawaz Sharif faced a serious confrontation with the Judiciary and the Executive, which eventually led to the resignation of President Leghari on December 2, 1997.

It was during this term that Pakistan carried out its *nuclear tests on May 28, 1998*, in response to the Indian experiments of its five nuclear devices. The Nawaz Government had found it imperative for Pakistan to carry out these nuclear tests, in order to provide an effective defense, and to deter Indian adventurism.

Nawaz Sharif also signed an accord with the government of PHILIPPINES for the peaceful use of Atomic energy. On 23rd of March 1997, the summit conference of OIC took place in Islamabad. Government also announced a new trade policy and allowed import of raw materials from India. First Women University was also established in Rawalpindi in January 1999. Bus service also began between India and Pakistan. Motorway project was also completed during the second term of Nawaz Sharif.

The Fifteenth Amendment was presumed to be an effort by Nawaz Sharif to acquire additional powers for himself. Soon a serious conflict and confrontation emerged on the scene between him and the Military Generals. This confrontation led to the resignation of General Jehangir Karamat on October 7, 1998. General Karamat was replaced by **General Pervez Musharraf.**

The Kargil Operation in its aftermath again led to tense relations between Nawaz ShSarif and the armed forces. This tension culminated into the removal of Nawaz Government by General Pervez Musharraf on October 12, 1999, thus bringing to an end the second term of Nawaz Sharif's Government.

Expected Questions:

Question No.1: What was the Pucca Qila Massacre? (4)   June 2010 Q.5 a

Question No.2: Why did Benazir Bhutto fall from office in 1990? (7)   Nov.2010 Q. 5 b

Question No.3: What problems did nawaz Sharif face as Prime Minister during the 1990s? (4)   June 2011 Q.5 a

Question No.4: Why did General Mushraff come to power in 1999? (7) Nov.2011 Q.5 b

Question No.5: Benazir Bhutto's government had to deal with accusations of encouraging corruption when she was in office in the late 1980s. Faced with increasing opposition to her rule, she was dismissed from office in 1990 by the President Ghulam Ishaq Khan. Nawaz Sharif became Prime Minister. He believed he could solve Pakistan's problems and move away from the corruption accusations of the previous government. However, he did encounter a number of problems, one of which was regarding the Co-operative societies.

(a) What was the Co-operative societies scandal? [4]   June 2014 Q.4 a

Question No.6: During the 1980s, relations between India and Pakistan were fraught with difficulties. The situation in Kashmir was far from resolved and both sides were developing nuclear weapons. Neither side was willing to sign the Nuclear Proliferation Treaty. By the 1990s tension was increasing again regarding nuclear weapons and Kashmir. Eventually an attempt was made to reduce tensions between the two countries by ending nuclear testing, and then the Kargil Conflict happened.

(a) What was the Kargil Conflict? (4)   June 2014 Q.5 a

Question No.7: Benazir Bhutto described her time as Prime Minister as problematic: 'I found that people opposed me simply on the grounds that I was a woman. The clerics took to the mosque saying that Pakistan had thrown itself outside the Muslim world by voting for a woman, that a woman had taken a man's place in an Islamic society. My opponents reduced themselves to verbal abuse rather than discuss issues simply because I was a woman.'
(a) Describe the problems caused by family feuds that faced the Benazir Bhutto governments. [4]   Nov. 2014 Q.5 a

Topic31

PAKISTAN'S FOREIGN RELATIONS:

UNITED NATIONS ORGANIATION:

The United Nations Organization has the following important organs:

1.   General Assembly

2.   Security Council

3.   Economic and Social Council

4.   Trusteeship Council

5.   Secretariat International Court of Justice

General Assembly:

It is the meeting place of 190 members of the UNO. Each country has one vote, but 5 members can represent a country. The General Assembly meets once or twice a year, but emergency meetings can be called any time. The main functions of the General Assembly are approving of the budget, supervising the activities of all departments and granting membership to new entrants.

Security Council:

The Security Council is the most important organ because its primary responsibility is to maintain world peace. It has 15 members of which 5 members are permanent (USA, USSR, UK, France and China), and 10 other members are elected for 2-year term. The permanent members have veto power. The Security Council orders ceasefire between two fighting countries and tries to hold talks between them. Security Council can impose economic boycott if a country refuses t o accept UN resolutions.

Economic and Social Council:

This council is concerned with economic, social cultural, educational and health affairs of the member nations. The council has 54 members elected for 3 years and it holds its meetings at least twice a year. It coordinates the functions of UNCESCO, ILO and WHO.

Trusteeship Council:

It is not functioning now.

Secretariat: It is the headquarters of the UNO and has a large number of offices of the Organization. About 14000 workers work in these offices, Secretary General is the chief administrative officer. The members of the secretariat are not allowed to get instructions from any government nor supposed to be influenced by any country.

The Secretary General is elected by the General Assembly for a period of 5 years and can seek re-election. He has often to mediate between two nations, investigate disputes and try to respond to international crises.

International Court of Justice:

This court peacefully resolves legal disputes between two states. It has 15 judges drawn from member states elected for 9-year term by the General Assembly. All disputes brought before the court are decided by majority vote.

ORGANIZTION OF ISLAMIC CONFERENCE (OIC):

The Organization of Islamic Conference (OIC) was founded in August 1969 when the Jews set fire to a part of Al-Aqsa mosque in Jerusalem. Muslims all over the world were greatly irritated and felt that effective steps should be taken to protect the Islamic countries from the aggressive forces and they realized that the unity of the Muslim countries was essential. It was decided to hold a conference of the heads of all the Muslim countries to discuss the threat faced by the Muslim World. The first Summit Conference of OIC was held at Rabat (Morocco) in September

1969. The Middle East situation was discussed in detail. The Second summit conference was held at Lahore (Pakistan) in February 1974. Besides the discussion on Palestine problem and condemnation of Jewish aggression, a committee was formed for the elimination of poverty, illiteracy and disease from the Islamic countries. It was decided to set up an Islamic Development Bank for the help of needy countries.

Nine Islamic Summit Conferences have been held so far. The last one was in Qatar in 2000. In all these summit meetings the issues discussed are: The Middle East and Palestine Problem, Kashmir problem, Afghan problem, Iraq-Iran war, and Iraq's invasion of Kuwait. Israel's aggression was strongly condemned and it was demanded that Israel should withdraw from the Arab territories and Palestinians should be given a chance to form a state of their own

The Conference also aimed at the advancement of cultural, scientific, educational and trade interests of all Islamic countries and to create a spirit of cooperation amongst them in all these spheres. Establishment of trade centers and shipping organization was also taken up. In this way the OIC projects the feelings, sentiments and demands of the Muslim world.

But, sad to say, that real unity does not exist among the Muslim countries. At the Summit Conferences speeches are made, resolutions are passed, plans and schemes are approved but no practical step is taken. Every proposal seems to be   on paper. There has hardly been any positive or tangible achievement of OIC.

INDIA PAKISTAN RELATIONS:

India is the closest neighbor of Pakistan sharing a common border of over 2000 Kms from Arabian Sea to the mountains of Kashmir. But their relations have been tensing and strained right from the time of partition because of three main reasons.

Firstly, the Congress leaders never wanted the partition of the subcontinent. Therefore, they created every hindrance for the state of Pakistan. Unfair and unjust methods were adopted in the division of assets in order to destabilize Pakistan. Large scale planned massacre of Muslims in East Punjab and Delhi created massive refugee problem for Pakistan. Canal water dispute was created. Relations have been of unfriendliness and mistrust from the very beginning.

Secondly, the problem of Kashmir has poisoned the relations. War broke out in 1948 and in 1965 over this issue. After the 1965 war both countries signed the Tashkent Agreement, but they again clashed in 1971 when India gave a severe blow to Pakistan through military intervention in former East Pakistan and Bangladesh was created. This was followed by Shimla Agreement. But the basic problem of Kashmir remained unsolved. Thirdly, India is a large country which is much ahead of Pakistan in industry, technology and military strength. Therefore, India wants to dominate over all neighboring countries including Pakistan and wants to impose her will on them. India adopts a stubborn attitude in all matters and disregards treaties and agreements at her free will.

The Indus Water Treaty 1960 was an important agreement. It helped Pakistan to solve her canal water problem. But India started building Wular Dam and Salal Dam on Jhelum and Chenab rivers which was against the Indus Water Treaty.

During 1980s, when Russian forces invaded Afghanistan, relations became more strained because India sided with Russia while Pakistan supported Afghan Mujahidin who were fighting against Russian forces.

In September 1981, a no war pact was suggested by Pakistan but India did not agree. Dangers of military attack on Pakistan and on her nuclear installations were averted by diplomatic steps. In 1988 an agreement was signed for not attacking each other's nuclear installations. Another agreement was signed in 1991 to supply advance information about military exercises, troop's movement and on prevention of air space violations.

On the other hand, the public of both countries has a keen desire of good relations. There have been strong cultural relations between the two countries. Cricket and hockey matches are played. Singers and artists exchange visits. Pilgrims of one country visit sacred places in the other country. Divided families are eager to visit their relatives.

Pakistan has always expressed her intentions to have friendly relations with India and wants to solve all problems through peaceful negotiations. It is clear that without solving the Kashmir problem all efforts of lasting peace and friendly relations would be fruitless.

PAKISTAN AND MUSLIM COUNTRIES:

A good and brotherly relation with Muslim countries has been the corner stone of Pakistan's foreign policy from the very beginning. Muslim countries were given top priority in our foreign relations. Pakistan has enjoyed good relations with almost all the countries of the Islamic World because Islam is the common bond of brotherhood. There are great similarities in way of life, food, dress, customs, and religious festivals in almost all Muslim countries.

Very cordial and close cultural and religious relations have existed between Pakistan and **Iran**. Persian language had a deep impact on Urdu language and literature. Classes for teaching of Persian language were started at many places in Pakistan. Many Pakistani pilgrims visit the sacred tombs and shrines in Iran on regular basis.

Deep cultural and religious bonds have developed between Pakistan and **Saudi Arabia**. Hundreds of thousands of pilgrims from Pakistan go for Hajj and Umra every year. Their impact is so deep that Urdu language is widely understood in

Saudi Arabia. Pakistani scholars go for higher studies in Islamic religion to Saudi universities. Similarly, Saudi students' study in Pakistani medical and engineering colleges. Saudi Cadets receive military training in armed forces academies of Pakistan on regular basis. Teaching of Arabic through TV and radio was introduced in Pakistan.

Pakistan, Iran and **Turkey** got bound together by RCD pact in 1964. RCD was later transformed into ECO which includes many Central Asian Republics as well.

Unbreakable cultural, linguistic and trade relations exist between Pakistan and its immediate neighbor **Afghanistan**. Pushto is spoken on both sides of the border and there is great cultural and ethnic similarity. Pakistan has always helped Afghanistan. Over 3 million Afghan refugees have been given shelter in refugee camps in Pakistan. All kind of help is being offered to them from 1980 till now. The Afghan public wishes to keep good relations but the Afghan government has kept hostile attitude towards Pakistan from the very beginning. It may be hoped that good relations will prevail when peace returns to Afghanistan with a stable government.

Very close cultural relations exist between Pakistan and **Gulf States.** Pakistani artists and singers regularly hold their cultural shows which the public thoroughly enjoys. Sharjah Cricket matches have been very popular and Pakistani sportsmen regularly take part in it. A large number of Pakistani are working in Gulf States and Saudi Arabia and are helping in economic development in these countries.

PAKISTAN AND BANGLADESH:

Bangladesh was created after a lot of hostilities when the former East Pakistan got separated in December 1971. In the beginning relations remained strained and Pakistan did not recognize Bangladesh for 2 years. It was on the occasion of the OIC Summit Conference at Lahore in Feb. 1974 that Pakistan recognized Bangladesh. Sheikh Mujeeb-ur-Rehman was called to attend the OIC Conference.

Proper diplomatic relations started in 1975 after the visit of Z. A. Bhutto to Bangladesh. Bangladesh demanded division of assets from Pakistan but did not agree to share any liabilities.

Communication link and air services were started in 1976. Close relations developed during the period of president Zia-ur-Rehman. Pakistan offered food and material assistance in 1985 and 1988 floods. In 1979 trade agreements were signed. Trade between the two countries has been steadily increasing. Bangladesh exports tea, jute and jute goods to Pakistan. Pakistan exports machinery, spare parts, and cloth and sports goods to Bangladesh. Bangladesh and Pakistan support each other on international forums. Bangladesh supports Pakistan on the Kashmir issue. Both are members of the SAARC organization under- which a number of agreements have been finalized for the promotion of trade, tourism and exchange of cultural programmers. Trade delegations of both countries exchange visits regularly and the trade between them has been gradually increasing,

PAKISTAN AND IRAN:

Iran is our neighboring country on the western side sharing a long boundary with Baluchistan. Rail, road and air links existed between the two countries from the very beginning. Iran was the first country to recognize Pakistan when it came into existence. Liaquat Ali Khan and King Raza Shah exchanged visits in 1950.

Very strong cultural ties existed between the two countries since medieval times. Persian was the court and official language for many centuries in India before the British brought the English language in 1835. Urdu language is deeply influenced by the Persian language.

Both Iran and Pakistan had leaning towards USA and the West and both joined the CENTO pact in 1954. Several trade agreements for trade and exchange of media information have taken place. In 1965, RCD was established and cultural and economic relations were strengthened. Now ECO has replaced RCD. Iran helped Pakistan during 1965 and 1971 crises. Iran always supported Pakistan on Kashmir issue.

During the Islamic revolution in Iran in 1979, relations became cool because Iran became very hostile towards USA. An Iranian diplomat was killed in Lahore which poisoned the relations between the two countries for some time. But relations improved greatly after a democratic government was set up in Iran. Both Iran and Pakistan decided to withdraw from the CENTO pact in 1979. Iran supported Pakistan during the Russian invasion of Afghanistan during 1979 - 1988 periods.

However, Iran remains our trusted ally and very cordial relations exist between the two countries.

PAKISTAN AND AFGHANISTAN:

Afghanistan is the immediate neighbor and shares a long border with Pakistan in the north-west. There have been strong historic bonds of religion, culture and language between the two countries. Kabul and Kandahar have been parts of Indian Kingdom during the Muslim and Mughal rule. Pushto speaking people live on both sides of the border which is called the Durand Line. Afghanistan is a land locked country and her foreign trade passes through Pakistan using the port of Karachi.

But the Afghan government has been hostile and unfriendly from the very beginning under the influence of Russia and India. Afghanistan opposed Pakistan's membership to United Nations in September 1947. She strongly supported the 'Pakhtoonistan' separatist movement which was a clear attempt to weaken and destabilize Pakistan. The Afghan government refused to accept the Durand Line as the international boundary line between the two countries. In spite of this Pakistan has been trying to establish good relations with the brotherly Muslim country. Gen. Iskandar Mirza in 1956 and later Ayyub Khan visited Kabul for this purpose.

Twice diplomatic relations were broken in 1955 and in 1961 when Pakistan Embassy in Kabul was attacked and damaged. However, relations were restored and normalized during Ayyub Khan's period and further improved during Z.A Bhutto's period. Afghanistan remained neutral during the 1965 and 1971 India-Pakistan wars. Z. A. Bhutto and King Zahir Shah exchanged visits, but soon King Zahir Shah was deposed and exiled in 1973. Sardar Daud also visited Pakistan. During the period of successive prime ministers of Afghanistan relations remained strained.

In December 1979, Russian forces invaded Afghanistan. The Afghanistan government was pro-Russian, but the people rose up and took up arms against the Russian forces. The Afghan-freedom fighters (Mujahideen) were given full and whole-hearted support by Pakistan with arms, supplies and training. Pakistan also gave shelter to over 3 million Afghan refugees on humanitarian grounds and they were housed in refugee camps near Peshawar and Quetta. Pakistan however had to pay heavy price for this. Soviet and Afghan planes bombed Pakistani territories several times and drug trafficking and proliferation of arms became common in Pakistan. Afghanistan was caught in civil war after the withdrawal of Russian troops. While Pakistan has been willing to develop good relations with any stable government in Afghanistan in future.

PALESTINIAN ISSUE:

The Palestine problem has been the cause of unrest for the entire Muslim world. The people and government of Pakistan continue with their support and have always acknowledged the right of the Palestinian people. Pakistan has always spoken strongly in favor of the Arab cause in the United Nations, the Security Council and at all other international forums such as NAM etc.

At all OIC meetings Pakistan has stressed for the protection of the rights and interests of the Palestinian people and has always pressed for a just and honorable solution of the problem. Pakistan has always demanded that Israel should vacate the occupied Arab territories and should stop its expansionist designs. Also, Israel should stop the killing of innocent Palestinian people.

During the Second OIC summit Conference at Lahore in 1974, the Israeli attitude was strongly condemned. It was demanded that Israel should withdraw from occupied Arab territories and the former status of Jerusalem should be restored. Pakistan recognizes the PLO as the true representative of the Palestinian people. Pakistan does not recognize the state of Israel and h a s never shown any intention to develop diplomatic relations with that- state.

PAKISTAN AND EGYPT:

Both Egypt and Pakistan had been under the influence of British rule. Therefore, good relations existed between the two countries in the beginning. Egypt became a democratic state in 1953 when King Farooq was deposed and General Najib came in power.

In 1956, war between Egypt and Britain took place on Suez Canal issue. Pakistan's support for Egypt was lukewarm because Pakistan had become a member of CENTO and SEATO organizations. Relations between the two countries deteriorated. There were other reasons of cold relations as well.

Egypt claimed to be the leader of Muslim world. With the emergence of Pakistan as the largest Islamic State, Egypt's claim of leadership was threatened.

Secondly, Jamal Naser, who came in power after Najib, was a believer of Arab nationalism. Naser was more inclined towards India and supported Indian point of view on Kashmir. Egypt abstained from voting in the UNO on Kashmir. Relations between the two countries improved during the period of Ayyub Khan who paid a visit to Cairo and Jamal Naser paid a visit to Pakistan in 1960. At the time of Arab-Israel war, Pakistan fully supported the Arab cause and supported Egypt.

Relations further improved when Anwar Sadaat attended the Second Islamic Summit Conference which was held at Lahore in 1974.

In fact, Egypt's close relations with USSR and India had affected the relations between the two countries.

However, relations improved during Zia-ul-Haq's period. Egypt's membership of OIC was suspended when Egypt signed the Camp David Accord with Israel to get back her territories. Egypt was isolated from the Muslim World. In 1984, through the efforts of Zia-ul-Haq, Egypt's membership of OIC was restored during the 4[the] Summit conference of OIC at Casablanca. Relations between the two countries have been friendly since then and delegations have exchanged visits. Egypt offered help to Pakistan for Afghan refugees.

PAKISTAN AND USSR:

Relations between Pakistan and USSR have remained strained from the very beginning. In 1950 Liaquat Ali Khan received an invitation to visit the U.S.S.R. But this visit did not take place and Liaquat Ali Khan visited USA instead. At this Russia got inclined towards India which caused great difficulties for Pakistan in later years. Relations further worsened when Pakistan entered into CENTO and SEATO pacts which were designed to check any possibility of Russian expansion. Russia openly supported India on Kashmir issue and also supported the Pakhtoonistan movement.

One of the most serious incidents in Soviet-Pakistan relations occurred in May 1960 when an American spy plane, known as U2, flew from an American airbase near Peshawar and was shot down while flying over

U.S.S.R. Russia gave a very stern warning to Pakistan.

In 1962 the India-China war helped to improve Pakistan's relations with Russia who was greatly annoyed by India's acceptance of arms from USA.

U.S.S.R agreed to give a loan of 150 million dollars to Pakistan for oil exploration. Trade agreements also took place.

Relations improved when President Ayyub Khan visited Russia in April 1965. After the India-Pakistan War of 1965, the Tashkent agreement was signed between the two countries through the efforts of Russian president. But during 1971 crisis Russia fully supported India with military assistance and Pakistan lost its Eastern Wing.

Z. A. Bhutto visited Russia in 1972 and relations improved. Russia helped Pakistan in setting up a steel mill at Karachi, which has been a great asset to Pakistan.

In December 1979 Russian troops invaded Afghanistan and relations between the two countries deteriorated badly after this because Pakistan was helping the Mujahideen who were fighting against the Russian troops. Russian planes bombed Pakistan territory in NWFP. Thus till 1988 Pakistan was not successful in having good relations with the U.S.S.R. However, after the withdrawal of Russian troops from Afghanistan in 1989 the relations have improved.

PAKISTAN, UNO AND UNITED STATES:

Pakistan was a newly born independent state, which emerged on the world map on 14 August 1947 as the largest Muslim country in the world.

Pakistan was eager to be recognized as a sovereign state by all nations of the world. Therefore, Pakistan wished to join the UNO as soon as possible.

From the very beginning Pakistan got involved in arguments for the rights of Kashmiris. It also raised the question of Hyderabad and Junagarh in the Security Council. Therefore, Pakistan's membership of UNO was essential. Pakistan also wanted to play its role in peace keeping in the world under the charter of the UNO, and was against any act of territorial aggression, colonialism, nuclear arms race and racial discrimination all over the world. With these purposes and ideals, Pakistan joined the United Nations in September 1947.

Close and good relations existed between Pakistan and USA from the very beginning; especially after Liaqat Ali Khan's visit to USA in 1950 the relations became cordial. Pakistan needed food grains and military equipment which USA could supply. On the other hand, USA wanted a supporter in the region against communism.

Therefore, in 1954 and 1955, Pakistan signed the SEATO and CENTO pacts which were meant to check Russian expansion. With the help of these pacts Pakistan received financial and military assistance from U.S.A.

Relations worsened in 1962 because USA gave huge military aid to Bharat against China. Pakistan's protests were of no avail. Relations also worsened because Pakistan turned to China in 1962 for friendship and Ayyub Khan made a visit to China. During the 1965 War, USA did not help Pakistan and instead stopped the usual aid. Relations gradually improved when Pakistan played an important role in bringing USA and China closer in 1969 during the period of Yahya Khan.

In 1971 crises again Pakistan received no help from USA, and in 1972 Mr. Bhutto left the SEATO pact.

In 1979, the American Embassy in Islamabad was attacked by a mob and relations worsened. This was the lowest point of Pakistan - USA relations. All American aid programmers were suspended or cancelled. Pakistan had to pay Rs.20 million by way of compensation. But soon after the relations improved when Russia attacked Afghanistan in December 1979. Pakistan supported and helped the Afghan freedom fighters (Mujahideen) who fought against Russian aggression. Massive military and financial aid came to Pakistan from USA for this purpose. But after the withdrawal of Soviet troops from Afghanistan, Pakistan's importance gradually decreased and American aid was also reduced. However, on the whole, Pakistan has been successful in having good relations with USA between 1947 and 1999.

PAKISTAN AND BRITAIN:

Pakistan maintained good and friendly relations with Britain because of the colonial attachment of more than 100 years. Pakistan joined SEATO and CENTO of which UK was a very important member. In 1965 Britain played an important role in finalizing an agreement to solve RANN OF KUTCH dispute with India. Britain remained neutral in 1965 war although it suspended sale of arms to Pakistan. Britain again remained neutral during 1971 crises and advised Pakistan to have a political solution. During the Afghan crisis the British government was firm in support of Pakistan and offered formidable financial assistance for Afghan refugees.

Britain gave much assistance in educational sector through the agency of British Council. Britain remains an important trading partner of Pakistan on account of old colonial links. For historic, economic and political reasons, Britain has remained a valuable ally of Pakistan between 1947 and 1988.

The Commonwealth is an organization of all the former British colonies including UK itself. It was a useful platform for states to exchange views. However, Pakistan withdrew from the commonwealth during Z. A. Bhutto's time on the point of recognition of Bangladesh. During the period of 1972- 1988 Pakistan remained cut off from the Commonwealth. But later Pakistan rejoined the Commonwealth during the time of Prime Minister Benazir Bhutto in 1989.

The richer Commonwealth countries have always supplied Pakistan with economic and technical aid. Government of Canada, New Zealand and Australia have been providing valuable financial and technical assistance to Pakistan. Substantial aid has been given to Pakistan for Wardak Project, Mania Dam and for development of railway and irrigation systems.

On the whole, Pakistan has been successful in having good relations with Britain and Commonwealth countries.

PAKISTAN AND CHINARELATIONSHIP:

Pakistan recognized the communist government of China in 1950 and supported it in regaining the UNO membership. During 1956-60, leaders of both countries visited each other's country to strengthen economic and cultural relations. In 1963, the boundary line between the two countries was demarcated to avoid any conflict in future. A series of trade agreements were signed in 1960s. China granted $60 million interest free loan and became the world's largest importer of Pakistan's cotton. Pakistan imported industrial machinery and developed the Heavy Mechanical Complex at Taxila. Pakistan International Airline started regular flights to China which resulted in increased business. Karakorum Highway is the road link that flourishes trade and tourism between the two countries. China has supported Pakistan's stand on Kashmir issue. During the 1965 war with India, China supplied military aid to Pakistan along with diplomatic assistance. In 1986, the two countries signed a nuclear cooperation treaty which is an indication of very good relations. China gave the Chashma Nuclear Power Plant to Pakistan, constructed near Mianwali and which started operation in 1999.

Now coming to the weaker side, Pakistan did not have good relations with China in its early few years after independence due to pro-American policies (USA and China were rivals). In 1959 Pakistan condemned military action in Tibet which was displeasure for China. In the 1971 war with India, China did not support Pakistan due to former USSR pressure that supported India. During 1990s China wanted Pakistan to resolve its issue of Kashmir with India. Perhaps she wanted a compromise which was a cause of resentment for Pakistan.

Conclusively, it can be said that as a whole Pakistan has maintained cordial relations with China. The two countries have been living in harmony. Delegations from almost all walks of life exchanged visits. Up to 1999, there were strong economic, trade and cultural ties between the two countries. And Pakistan received significant military and industrial equipment from China.

SAARC:

The **South Asian Association for Regional Cooperation (SAARC)** is an economic and geopolitical organization of eight countries that are primarily located in South Asia. The SAARC Secretariat is based in Kathmandu, Nepal. The combined economy of SAARC is the 3rd largest in the world in the terms of GDP. SAARC nations comprise 3% of the world's area and contain 21% (around 1.7 billion) of the world's total population. India makes up over 70% of the area and population among these eight nations. All non-Indian member states except Afghanistan share borders with India but only two other members, Pakistan and Afghanistan, have a border with each other.

The idea of regional political and economic cooperation in South Asia was first raised in 2 May 1980 by Bangladesh President Ziaur Rahman and the first summit was held in Dhaka on 8 December 1985, when the organization was established by the governments of Bangladesh, Bhutan, India, Maldives, Nepal, Pakistan, and Sri Lanka. Since then the organization has expanded by accepting one new full member, Afghanistan, and several observer members.

The SAARC policies aim to promote welfare economics, collective self-reliance among the countries of South Asia, and to accelerate socio-cultural development in the region. The SAARC has developed external relations by establishing permanent diplomatic relations with the EU, the UN (as an observer), and other multilateral entities. The official meetings of the leaders of each nation are held annually whilst the foreign ministers meet twice annually. The 18th SAARC Summit was held in Kathmandu from 26-27 November 2014.